CRYING OUT FOR

JUSTICE

FULL-THROATED AND
UNSPARINGLY

A Parish Priest's Story

CRYING OUT FOR

JUSTICE

FULL-THROATED AND
UNSPARINGLY

A Parish Priest's Story

TIM STIER

MILL CITY PRESS, MINNEAPOLIS

Mill City Press, Inc.
322 First Avenue N, 5th floor
Minneapolis, MN 55401
612.455.2293
www.millcitypublishing.com

ISBN-13: 978-1-63413-380-7
LCCN: 2015902381

Book Design by Lois Stanfield

Printed in the United States of America

CONTENTS

PROLOGUE

ON FRIDAY MORNING, March 19, 2004, I was sitting in my living room in the rectory/office of Corpus Christi Parish, Fremont, writing my Sunday homily when the parish secretary called from the parish office downstairs to tell me that Dan McNevin was there asking to see me.

I felt my heart race as my mind scrambled to understand the implications of this unexpected visit. Several weeks earlier I had received a call from Sister Barbara Flannery at the Oakland Diocese informing me that a story would soon be appearing in the local Fremont Argus newspaper detailing Dan McNevin's childhood sexual abuse at the hands of a former Corpus Christi pastor. Sister Barbara said that Dan had been to see her and that she believed his painful story. Before the story appeared, the reporter called me for my parishioners' possible reaction to Dan's abuse allegations. At the end of our phone interview, I asked the reporter to let Dan know I would like to meet him, never really expecting that he would show up at my doorstep at the very house where he was molested.

So I headed downstairs filled with trepidation to meet Dan McNevin in person. I invited him into the dining room, closed the doors, and for the next couple of hours listened to a story which would change my life in ways I could not have imagined. It is no exaggeration to write that I have not been the same since. Dan's humanity, honesty, and painful story led me to the hardest decision of my life.

This book is about that decision which has led me to a new way of living my Catholic faith. Dan's visit was the "straw that broke this camel's back" (see chapter 17) and he will forever be for me a hero in an historic struggle to reform the Catholic Church. What happened to Dan and to thousands of other children and teenagers throughout the world was criminal and imposed lifelong suffering on the survivors. Ten years later, I still grieve. Sadly, these crimes persist because the secretive clerical celibate culture persists.

INTRODUCTION

THE CATHOLIC CHURCH is suffering a leadership crisis of gargantuan proportions. As a priest in the Diocese of Oakland, California, for twenty-five years, I witnessed first-hand this crisis of leadership.

This book is the story of my early faith development, my experience as a parish priest from 1979 to 2004, and the ensuing years in voluntary exile from active priesthood up to the present. I have written this story to counteract a persistent and widely held myth that the problems in the Catholic Church are caused only by bad apples, e.g., priests who sexually abuse children, and bishops who repeatedly reassign these priests to different parishes where they abuse more children. There are indeed many bad apples among Catholic clergy but I am convinced that the Church's basic problem is structural in nature and that the problems plaguing the Church will continue until the crying need for structural reform is addressed. The problem is a bad barrel, not just bad apples. This structural reform will need to be multi-faceted addressing the evils of clergy sexual abuse, clericalism, sexism, chronic abuse of authority, secrecy, and the idolatry of putting the Church and its traditions ahead of God. At the root of all these problems is a failure of faith: faith in Jesus as head of the Church and thus the leader of leaders.

Many people keep waiting and hoping for things to improve in the Catholic Church thinking the next bishop or the next pope will lead meaningful reform efforts. Despite the hope engendered by the change of tone under Pope Francis, the main reason those hopes keep being dashed is that the structure itself blocks real reform from happening. The current monarchical structure inherited from the Middle Ages values secrecy, adherence to tradition, and extreme clericalism over transparency, innovation, and inclusion of lay people in decision-making. Structural reform is not only not considered; it's not even allowed to be discussed. Those in authority claim that the present structure is willed by God and may not be questioned. To question it is dissent, and dissent is punishable by silencing and excommunication.

It took many years for me to realize that the Church as it is presently structured is incapable of recognizing the need for structural reform. From the mid 1990's until 2005, I tried to initiate discussion among my brother priests and the bishop of the Oakland Diocese about the Church's problems, but whenever the discussion headed in the direction of the need for structural reform, the subject was changed or the discussion terminated.

I refused to believe that bishops and my fellow priests would not be open to discussing the priest shortage, the exclusion of women from the priesthood and leadership in the Church, the labeling of gay and lesbian people as intrinsically disordered, mandatory celibacy, and the sexual abuse of children and youth by clergy, in a completely open and unfettered way, but my naivete was slowly eroded by repeated encounters with denial and diversionary tactics. At those times when I would dig in my heels and refuse to be silenced, I would be told that it was not within our authority to deal with these issues.

There are no shortage of books and other publications addressing the crisis in the Catholic Church but I believe my story adds a unique perspective coming as it does from a parish priest who started out as a true believer, completely at home in the Catholic Church, who gradually realized that the Gospel of Jesus Christ was being compromised and undermined by the very institution designed to serve and proclaim that Gospel.

The stories that comprise this book are told in the hope of removing the blinders from many Catholics' eyes so that structural reform may occur soon and very soon. The credibility and relevance of the Catholic Church is at its lowest point in modern history and promises to get even lower with each successive revelation of scandal, betrayal of trust, and bankrupt dioceses. Structural change cannot happen as long as the laity remain unaware and apathetic.

In March, 2005, I told my bishop that I was choosing to go into voluntary exile from the priesthood until he was willing to open a public dialogue on the crisis facing the Church. He wasn't, and I did! The inspiration to give up my livelihood and public ministry came from the lives of people being crushed in faith and spirit by Church policies and structures. I could no longer in good conscience publicly represent an institution that oppressed abuse survivors, women, gay and lesbian people, and set up priests for failure by an outdated theology of priesthood and human sexuality. Now I "cry out, full-throated and unsparingly" (Isaiah 58, 1) on behalf of those "who dwell in darkness and the shadow of death" (Luke 1, 79) because to remain silent would be my undoing.

I am grateful you have chosen to read this book and hope it inspires you to join in the effort to structurally reform the Catholic Church in the service of Jesus and the Gospel.

Part I

A CHILD'S FAITH AND
TWENTY YEARS OF EDUCATION

Chapter One

BEGINNINGS

I WAS BORN IN OAKLAND, CALIFORNIA, in 1949, the third of five children. At the time, my father Victor was a newspaper reporter and my mother Audine a homemaker. They had met at UC Berkeley as undergraduates both majoring in English. My father was Catholic, my mother agnostic. Their marriage in 1942 had been difficult to accept for both sets of my grandparents because of the significant difference in religious outlook. But my parents were in love and my mother graciously agreed to be married in the Catholic Church and to allow my father to raise my siblings and me in the Catholic faith. This arrangement led to a less than typical Catholic upbringing for us children.

I was baptized at St. Theresa Parish in Oakland two months after my birth. My earliest memories of religious activity included Mass every Sunday, grace before meals, and bedtime prayers prayed kneeling at my bedside in the company of my father and my older brothers Kit and Mark. The prayers included an Our Father, Hail Mary, Act of Contrition and a Glory Be, followed by intercessory prayers for the sick and the dead. I can't remember ever not believing in God. Prayer in church and at home supported my simple faith. The rote nature of prayers only made me want to pray these holy words with whole-hearted fervor so I wouldn't sound rote to God. I believed God was listening to our prayers so I wanted to get them right.

Until age six, I lived in Oakland where I attended nursery school, kindergarten, and half of first grade. But in 1955, my dad quit his job with the Oakland Tribune newspaper and joined the United States Information Agency whose purpose was to educate and propagandize other countries about the good qualities of the U.S. over against the bad qualities of the Soviet bloc. Over the next twenty-five years, my journalist-turned- diplomat father would represent the United States in five foreign countries: Thailand, Greece, Sri Lanka, Finland, and the Netherlands. In late 1955, we moved to Bangkok, Thailand, traveling by way of propeller airplanes with stops in Honolulu, Guam, Wake Island, Manila, and Hong Kong. I recall attending Mass in Manila and feeling at home there because the Filipinos shared our Catholic faith.

In Bangkok I attended an American international school and a parish church run by Redemptorist priests from the U.S. working as missionaries in Thailand. Our parish was called Holy Redeemer or "Wat Roman", "wat" being a Buddhist name for a place of worship and "roman" a reference to the "Roman" Catholic Church. The church building resembled a Thai Buddhist wat, quite striking and beautiful. I celebrated by First Communion there in 1956 and my Confirmation in 1959.

It may have been the tropical climate in Thailand that induced my parents to have two more children during our stay there: Tracy was born in 1958 and Geoff in 1959. Their arrivals to our family brought us all immense joy. Both were baptized at Holy Redeemer/Wat Roman. I loved the fact that my mother joined us for those really special church occasions. I didn't understand why she didn't attend Mass with us on Sundays nor pray with us at home. I'm guessing there was an unspoken rule that we were not supposed to ask about my mother's non-participation in our family's religious activities. All I know is that I was happy that she attended the really big celebrations; I was equally happy that when we returned home from regular Sunday morning Mass, a big breakfast was awaiting us.

I rather enjoyed going to Mass on Sundays. Mass at that time was still in Latin so my father got each of us a missal, the book with all the Mass prayers in Latin and English. The missal, with its colored ribbons to mark the pages and with some sections printed in red ink to indicate rubrics (rules of worship), fascinated me. Having my own copy of a missal helped enhance my sense of participation and interest.

The Thai people we knew and lived among were almost exclusively Buddhist. Buddhist monks in orange robes would stop by our house fairly regularly to literally beg for rice and vegetables for the food bowls they carried. We would oblige them whenever possible. I was intrigued by these peaceful men with shaven heads who seemed so gentle and kind. We visited many Buddhist temples in my childhood containing impressive statues of Buddha: reclining buddhas, seated buddhas, and standing buddhas. We had Buddhist art in our home. I found Thai people to be invariably, kind, friendly and peaceful. Only later in life did I connect the kindness of Thai people with their Buddhist faith. I left Bangkok with a good feeling about Buddhism based on my experience of the Thai people, monks, wats, statues, shrines and other holy places. I'm grateful for those early experiences of inculturation into Thai Buddhism. Many years later when the Catholic Church opened up to eastern religions, it was easy for me to see how compatible Christianity and Buddhism are.

In 1960, my father was transferred to Athens, Greece. Before moving to Athens, we took a driving tour through Italy, France and Spain. I was moved by the many signs of Catholicism in Italy and Spain and by all the Christian art in museums such as the Louvre in Paris and the Prado in Madrid. My faith was strengthened by these signs of Christianity among peoples and places far from home. I recall feeling excited as we visited Castel

Gandolfo, the Pope's summer residence outside Rome. Pope Pius XII appeared on his balcony to bless my family and the rest of the crowd. Travelling abroad taught me how historically rooted the Catholic Church is and how universal as well. Because of those experiences, I felt proud to be Catholic. That pride increased as I learned in catechism classes that the Catholic Church was "the one true church" because it traced its leadership, the Pope and the bishops, directly back to Jesus and the Apostles.

The tradition of Sunday Mass provided me a sense of stability and rootedness in my life, a life that was otherwise so full of change and dislocation. Even while travelling in foreign countries, my dad would make sure we found a church for Sunday Mass. God and Church became my anchors, always available wherever I found myself. During our time in Athens which lasted five years, I became an altar server. Although my brother Mark and I resisted memorizing the Latin Mass responses, eventually we mastered our parts. I felt needed at Sunday Mass because of my special role, my closeness to the altar, my distinctive clothing of cassock and surplice, and my immersion in the ritual with its colors, candles, bells, movement, body postures, and mysterious holy language. Our parish in Athens consisted of a chapel that as far as I knew was only used on Sundays for the few Catholics in the area. There was also a Catholic Cathedral in downtown Athens but we never attended Mass there.

In Athens, there were two schools available to English speaking students: an American community school which my older brothers attended, and a small Catholic school run by Ursuline nuns from the U.S. which I attended 6th through 9th grades. One of the nuns, Mother Stanislaus, made a positive impact on me by her kindness, gentleness and personal interest in me. In those days, Ursuline sisters were addressed as "mother", not "sister". These dedicated women made a lasting impression on me for I remember all their names: the aforementioned Mother

Stanislaus, and Mothers Cornelius, Daniel Joseph, and Carol Ann. I find it ironic in retrospect that religious women of that era would choose male names to mark their religious commitment. A male name carried more weight than a female name. I thought nothing of it at the time but now in light of the clearly second place status of women in the Church, I feel saddened by the need of these women to adopt male names. After Vatican II (1962–1965, Mother Stanislaus became Kathleen again, her given name at baptism. A redemption of sorts at last!

For 10th grade my parents decided to send me to a Catholic boarding school in Rome called The Notre Dame International School for Boys run by the Brothers of the Holy Cross. We heard about the school through a friend of mine in Athens who had been attending it for a couple of years. My parents were not entirely happy with the American community school in Athens so they chose to invest in my education by sending me away to Rome.

My one year at The Notre Dame International School was a mixed experience for me. I liked the fact that it was run by religious brothers but I suffered some cultural shock by being away from home for the first time in my life in a foreign city with yet another foreign language. Classes were conducted in English but many of my classmates spoke some Italian. The faculty was a mixture of Holy Cross Brothers and lay teachers. I enjoyed the adventure of walking around Rome on weekends and the occasional field trips to other parts of Italy. I enjoyed the Italian food in our school cafeteria and the camaraderie of many of my classmates. In particular, I liked my three roommates, all of whose fathers worked in the oil industry in Benghazi, Libya. I continued to enjoy Mass but found the presiding priest uninspiring. He seemed pious but way too serious and dull.

I was in school in Rome for the 1964–1965 school year which coincided with the last session of the Second Vatican

Council. In spite of the tremendous impact the Council would have on my later life, I was unaware of its existence at the time it was happening and in the very city where it was happening. In June of 1965 I returned home to Athens. Later that summer, my father was transferred to Washington, D.C.

Leaving Athens on August 11th was the saddest day of my life to that point. I remember the date vividly because it was the day I had to part from my first true love. Her name was Susan and we had fallen in love the summer after my 9th grade. Her father, also a diplomat, was assigned to Athens after an assignment in Cairo, Egypt. I had remembered Susan from 1st grade in Bangkok because I had had a crush on her even then. When I heard that Susan and her family were moving to Athens, I was very curious to meet her. She had developed into a pretty and charming young woman and we hit it off right away. She attended the American community school in Athens for her 10th grade while was I was shipped off to Rome for mine.

That summer of 1965 was magical as Susan and I grew very close. She joined my family on a short visit to the island of Crete, and I travelled with her family to another Greek island. Her home was walking distance from ours so I would frequently hang out at her house. I remember our first date during which we attended an outdoor movie. I spent most of the movie working up the courage to put my arm around her. When I finally did, I was delighted to find that she was fine with that. At 15, I was innocent and awkward, and clueless about girls.

When August 11th arrived, Susan came down to the port of Athens to see us off. I was feeling utterly desolate at the prospect of leaving her. Once the ship embarked, I could not hold back my tears so I went off by myself for a good cry so my brothers and sister wouldn't see me weeping. I was experiencing my first real taste of grief and the emotions that came with it were overwhelming and unwelcome.

In retrospect, the five years I lived in Athens from age 11 to 15 were magical. I fell in love there and that love was reciprocated; I realized that I had some talent as a baseball player; I gained an appreciation for ancient history through the art and ruins of ancient Greece; I luxuriated in the clear, blue waters of the Aegean Sea and enjoyed the incomparable taste of Greek tomatoes and olives. All in all, not a bad place to grow up.

Chapter Two

HIGH SCHOOL AND COLLEGE
IN WASHINGTON, D.C.

WE SETTLED IN HOT AND MUGGY WASHINGTON, D.C. in the summer of 1965 but my heart was still in Athens pining for Susan. She and I exchanged letters three times a week for a few months to get us through the pain of those first few months apart. Meanwhile my two older brothers Kit and Mark had moved away and I started 11th grade at Woodrow Wilson High School in northwest Washington. It was a much larger school than I was used to and I didn't know a soul. I found the first few months an awkward time of adjustment. That spring, I tried out for the school baseball team and made the varsity, a development which did wonders for my self-esteem and social life. Susan and I still corresponded but we agreed that dating other people would be permissible if not welcome.

My father and I along with my two younger siblings began attending Blessed Sacrament Parish close to our home and I was inspired by the homilies there of a Father Rogan. He preached in a way that related the Scripture readings to life and he presented us with a Jesus who was fully human, compassionate, wise, just and loving. The other priests' homilies weren't horrible, just boring and long. I was always thrilled when it was Fr. Rogan who walked out to begin Mass on a given Sunday. He awakened in me a hunger and appreciation for the preached Word of God.

By 1965, the Mass was celebrated in English, a change which I welcomed. I don't recall us getting involved in that parish in any way beyond attending Sunday Mass. This was typical of my family in part because my mother is not Catholic. My dad explained to me years later that he didn't think it right to attend parish events if it meant my mother not participating.

I continued to pray on my own before bedtime but my prayer life hadn't grown much beyond a child's way of praying. The main connection between my prayer and life was an awareness of sin and asking God to forgive my sins. My knowledge of God was vague and ill-defined but Sunday Mass kept Jesus and the Scriptures in my awareness and I was drawn to both. I remember a special attraction to the Last Gospel, a part towards the end of the pre-Vatican II Latin Mass in which the prologue of the Gospel of John (chapter one) was read. I loved that passage and was continuously drawn to its mysterious description of Jesus as the Word of God made flesh who came to make his dwelling place with the human race. How good is that!, I thought. My early attraction to the Gospel would later bloom into a life-long love affair and be the prime motivation for my decision to become a priest.

My primary interests though were certainly not God and church. I loved sports, particularly baseball, but also football, basketball, tennis and golf. I loved girls and enjoyed the company of different girls to school dances, parties and on dates. My heart though was still committed to Susan with whom I continued to correspond my junior and senior years. I never felt completely at home at Woodrow Wilson High School in part because I was an introverted teenager and in part because I didn't share the rootedness of many of the other students who had lived in the D.C. area all their lives. I always felt a little like a stranger. Church on Sunday continued to be an anchoring experience for me as the rituals, Scriptures and intermittently good preaching nourished my attraction to God.

My self-esteem in high school was mixed in spite of the ego boost of making the varsity baseball team. I was an average student who didn't work very hard. My parents and teachers told me I could do better but I lacked the motivation to study harder. I made friends fairly easily but I was a bit surprised when people liked me. Girls thought I was cute and that was flattering to know. A group of jocks invited me to join their fraternity but I backed off after a painful hazing experience which involved being blindfolded, driven to the outskirts of town, and beaten with a wooden paddle. As much as I wanted to belong, I decided enduring cruelty wasn't worth the indignity and humiliation. From my earliest years, I had a soft spot for the outsider, the unpopular, and the suffering. I would make a point to be kind to fellow students who didn't fit in or who were marginalized for being different or odd. And so my better nature opted out of the fraternity with its ritualized cruelty. At the time I felt cowardly and humiliated. Only in retrospect did I feel gratitude for that choice.

My relationship with my parents was benign most of the time. My older brothers and father often quarreled. My dad loved us deeply but he tended to moralize and overemphasize grades and intellectual achievement. He would get angry at my brothers but could never admit or own his anger. He taught us that "gentlemen don't get angry." I hated friction in the family so I unconsciously took on the role of the joker and the good son who didn't cause trouble for my parents. We as a family didn't share much on an emotional level so I often felt lonely with my doubts, insecurities and sadness. I appeared happy and carefree but inside I often felt alone and disconnected from others. I suffered self-doubt and worried about what my future would bring. I distracted myself from these feelings by listening to baseball games on the radio which was a thrill second only to actually playing the game. My love affair with baseball continues to this day.

In June, 1967, I graduated from high school. That summer I worked on a passenger ship out of San Francisco to Asia and back while fretting over which college to attend. In my family, there was no question about attending college. It was expected, and my parents paid the tuition. I settled at the last minute on The George Washington University (GW) in Washington, D.C., a liberal arts school of about 13,000 students.

At GW I studied International Affairs and earned a BA in 1971. My freshman year, I lived at home. Then my parents moved to Sri Lanka so I lived with a high school friend's family my sophomore year and in apartments in D.C. and Arlington my junior and senior years. Throughout my college years I continued to attend Mass on Sundays because it felt like home and always in the hope that I would be touched by God there, which from time to time I was.

My girl friend Susan from my Athens' days moved back to the States and attended college in Connecticut. We resumed our close relationship and managed to spend a weekend with each other about once a month. By our junior year, we realized we lacked enough in common to continue our exclusive relationship so Susan had the courage to break it off. I grieved our parting deeply but knew it was the right decision. As a practicing Catholic, I was never completely comfortable with the fact that Susan and I had an intimate relationship. I used to confess this sin regularly in order to receive Communion so our breakup brought with it the silver lining of a less guilty conscience. I missed Susan terribly but gradually started dating again.

My first two years at GW, I earned a C average. I was so disgusted by my mediocre grades that I wrote to my parents in Sri Lanka promising them that if I did not improve my grade point average my junior year, I would not accept any more tuition money from them. I changed my study habits by retreating to an isolated desk in the stacks of the college library for daily study sessions: no radio, TV, friends, or other distractions. Coincidentally my classes became smaller and more interesting and I maintained a B+ average my last two years at GW. I earned some extra spending money by working as a part-time checker at the Safeway store on the basement level of the Watergate Apartment building near campus. It was hard work and hard on the feet with all the time spent standing at the checkout counter but I met a fascinating variety of people and made some good friends among my fellow employees.

During the summers of my college years, I was able to visit my parents in Sri Lanka and Finland at government expense since I was still a dependent of my parents. I loved the time I spent in both those countries, one hot and humid, the other cold and dry. When I first arrived in Sri Lanka in the summer of 1969, my father organized a party to introduce me to all my parents' Sri Lankan friends. Sri Lankan names can be long and challenging for a non Sri Lankan to pronounce, so I was very impressed when my dad introduced me to all the guests by their first and last names. I later asked him how he could manage those tough names. He told me that he was blessed with a good memory but that he also worked hard at remembering people by name.

Later that fall after I had returned to the United States for my junior year at GW, my father was in his office one day in Colombo, Sri Lanka, when an American monk walked in and introduced himself as "Tom Merton" and asked my father to help him locate a Buddhist monk Merton wanted to meet. Thomas Merton had written a best selling autobiography, THE SEVEN STOREY MOUNTAIN, in the 1940's and became the most widely read Catholic author and poet of the mid twentieth century. My father was absolutely thrilled by Merton's surprise visit, so much so that he invited him over to the house to meet the family and a few friends. Tom obliged and enchanted all in attendance with his story-telling, humor, and humanity. Merton was on leave from Gethsemane Abbey in Kentucky to attend a Catholic-Buddhist conference in Bangkok. I had grown up hearing my father talk about Merton's books.

I share that story about my father's interest in Merton to show how my father's deep Catholic faith was rooted in and supported by serious study and intellectual conviction. It wouldn't be long before I realized that I shared that same penchant for God-seeking by way of the intellect. My dad was also a great admirer of Dorothy Day and the Catholic Worker movement. He corresponded with her over the years and once during a visit by her to northern California, my parents drove Dorothy to an event. My father loved Dorothy because of her pro labor activities, her faith, and the philosophy that undergird the Catholic Worker.

My senior year of college, I took a course called the History of Western Political Theory which traced the development of democratic ideas from the ancient Greeks through Western Europe to the United States. I studied the writings of theorists like Rousseau and Locke whose ideas helped lay the foundations for some of the key principles in the U.S. Constitution. As enlightening as this world of ideas was to me, I found myself hungering for something even deeper and more satisfying to help me understand myself and our world. I couldn't imagine making a living at political science or international relations but my study of those subjects deepened my desire for knowledge and truth.

I graduated from GW in the summer of 1971 without a clue of what to do with the rest of my life. Unfortunately, the military draft lottery assigned me a low number which meant I would soon be drafted into military service for two years. All of a sudden the Vietnam War had my full attention. Once I passed the physical required for military service, I enlisted in the Army rather than waiting to be drafted. I didn't want to spend two years in the military, particularly during an unpopular war, but I felt obligated to do my duty to my country.

Chapter Three

MILITARY SERVICE AT
WEST POINT, NEW YORK

ENTERING THE U.S. ARMY in war time as a two year enlistee meant that I could be sent anywhere my superiors dictated. I enlisted in Oakland, attended Basic Training for eight weeks at Fort Ord on the Monterey Peninsula, followed by eight more weeks of military police training at Ft. Gordon in Augusta, Georgia. I was assigned to MP training in part because I had a college degree. The Army was upgrading its police force at a time when civilian police forces were doing upgrades throughout the country. After MP training, I was assigned as an enlisted man to the Military Police force at the U.S. Military Academy at West Point, New York. Once arrived, I volunteered to be a desk clerk in the First Sergeant's office in order to avoid shift work with my fellow MP's. Shift work entailed switching from day shift to swing shift to night shift every two weeks, a recipe for chronic sleep deprivation. As a desk clerk, I worked Monday through Friday, 8 to 5, with weekends off except during football season when I helped direct traffic for Army home football games.

West Point is located approximately fifty miles upstate from New York City in a hilly, scenic valley along the west bank of the Hudson River. I lived in the MP barracks but had access to most cadet facilities such as the golf course, ski slope, gym and track. I played on the MP softball team, became a jogger through the good influence of a fellow desk clerk, and enjoyed many weekend trips to New York City for baseball games, plays, and other diversions.

I attended the Catholic parish up the hill from my barracks and loved both priests there. They were good preachers and Mass most Sundays was a nourishing experience. One of the priests invited parishioners to an evening series to listen to tapes of Father Hans Kung, the famous Swiss theologian. After each tape, the priest moderated a discussion on Kung's teachings about the Second Vatican Council. Father Kung's talks fascinated me and sparked a desire to learn more. I was beginning to understand that Catholicism involved more than Sunday Mass.

Meanwhile, in the barracks just over a wooden divider from my bed and locker, lived a fellow MP named Jack. Jack was a joyful and deeply committed born-again Christian. He noticed that I would walk up the hill each Sunday morning for Mass so he began to question my commitment to Catholicism. He had been raised nominally Catholic but told me he only came to faith in Jesus in a Bible-based church. Jack was critical of Catholicism without being insulting or mean-spirited. He was sincere and articulate in his Christian faith and invited me to attend a Bible study with him, which I did a few times. I found Jack's criticism of Catholicism suspect but I did not know enough to refute what he was saying. Jack's challenges to my Church turned out to be the catalyst that inspired me to study my faith tradition in depth. I started going to the West Point library at night and reading up on Catholic tradition, doctrine, spirituality, history and theology.

I also became friends with a part-time secretary at the parish named Rita and through her got to know the pastor, Fr. McCormick. He was a deep thinker and an excellent preacher. I also started dating Rita's college- age daughter, a friendship that lasted many years after my twenty month long stay at West Point.

My Army term ended in October of 1973. I was then 24 years old and still uncertain about what to do with the rest of my life. I drove back to California and for lack of a better idea, enrolled in a Master's Degree program in political science at Cal State University in Hayward. I didn't have much money so my brother Kit and his wife Diane graciously let me live with them in Oakland so I could devote myself to being a full-time student. I attended St. Augustine, a parish near their house, and volunteered as a lector. The first time I read the Scriptures at Sunday Mass, I was so nervous my knees felt like jelly and my voice quavered. Proclaiming God's Word was nerve-wracking but profoundly rewarding. As a result of it of getting involved as a lector, something happened that changed the direction of my life.

Chapter Four

A RELIGIOUS EXPERIENCE

ONE DAY AFTER SUNDAY MASS, Michael Scanlon, the lector co-ordinator, invited me to join other men of the parish for the an-nual men's retreat at San Damiano Retreat in Danville, a suburb east of Oakland. I initially declined citing homework as an excuse. I didn't really understand what a retreat was and it sounded way too religious anyway. But Mr. Scanlon wasn't taking "no" for an answer. He persisted until I caved in just to get him off my back.

San Damiano is run by the Franciscan religious order and sits atop a hillside overlooking a scenic valley with a spectacular view of Mt. Diablo. The kind of retreat I attended is called a "preached retreat". The retreat masters, in this case two elderly Franciscan priests, would read a Bible passage and then offer a teaching on it geared to daily life concerns and spiritual renewal. The theme of my retreat was the Beatitudes as found at the beginning of chap-ter five of MATTHEW'S Gospel. After each teaching session, we were encouraged to go off by ourselves to reflect and pray on what we'd heard.

I cannot exaggerate the effect that preaching and teaching on the heart of Jesus' message had on me. I was astonished by the truth and beauty of the Gospel and the person of Jesus. The Gos-pel that I'd heard every Sunday of my life came alive for me that weekend in a way I could never have imagined. I felt excited and fearful about this truly good news about almighty God revealing him/herself as fully human, profoundly compassionate, tenderly merciful, and wanting to be MY friend. I thought to myself: I will never be the same, and I wondered: what do I do with this wonderful knowledge? After one of the retreat talks, I went to speak with one of the priests to tell him what I was experiencing. I told him that Jesus' message of truth and love was more life-giving and significant than all the theories and philosophies I'd studied to that point. The wise old priest in his Franciscan habit suggested that I might have a vocation to the priesthood but that I would need to test that possibility in the following ways: pray about it, ask my family and friends if they could imagine me as a priest, and to take time to patiently discern what God was asking of me. Finally, he suggested I meet with the vocations director of the Diocese of Oakland.

My first reaction was, ME, a priest? No way! Priests are holy men who had never used profanity, never had sex, and never tried pot, all of which I had done. I could not imagine myself as a priest, yet I couldn't deny the profound impression my encounter with Jesus had on me. He calls blessed the "poor in spirit": those who don't have it all figured out, and those who sometimes feel alienated, alone, broken and insecure. He calls blessed those who grieve and feel sorrow. He calls blessed those who hunger for justice, for fairness, and for peace. And all of this teaching reflects the mind and heart of God. This teaching struck me as utterly true and utterly subline. Unable to ignore what had happened to me, I made an appointment with the vocations director, Fr. Jerry Kennedy.

I met with Fr. Jerry at his office in the chancery on Lakeshore Ave. in Oakland. His calm and friendly manner eased my fears. He asked me about my family and education as well as my motivation for coming to see him about the priesthood. To my surprise, he was very encouraging and affirming of my interest and motivation. He was the first but not the last to shatter my illusions about priesthood. Fr. Jerry was down to earth and related to me as his equal. Best of all, he affirmed my strong sense of being called to serve Jesus in the Church.

That fall, I entered the college seminary in Mountain View, south of San Francisco, to study philosophy for a year prior to beginning theological studies at St. Patrick's Seminary in Menlo Park. Father Jerry had offered me the choice of going directly to St. Patrick's and thus bypassing a year at the college seminary studying philosophy, but I welcomed an extra year to figure out if life as a priest was for me. I'd been pleasantly surprised when I passed the psychological tests required of all prospective seminary candidates. My low self-esteem kept getting challenged by positive feedback and I welcomed this surprising affirmation.

My encounter with Jesus at San Damiano mediated by the teaching and preaching of two Franciscan priests on the Beatitudes was a life altering experience. For me it was a personal discovery of "the pearl of great price", and the "hidden treasure", images in the parables of Jesus about how life changing it is to discover the Kingdom of God. I was willing and able to leave all behind to follow Jesus with loving devotion. Ever after, I warned people going on retreat to be careful because God might surprise them and change the direction of their lives forever. In spite of all the ups and downs I experienced in the ensuing years, that Jesus experience at San Damiano has never left me and my faith in him as Savior and Divine Friend anchors my life to this day. I believe that God continually pursues us to win our hearts. Sadly, we often miss that loving invitation because we are too busy, too distracted, or have our hearts set on treasures that fail to deliver on their promises. For Jesus' calling to take root and grow in me, I needed formation, study and discipline, the next part of my journey.

Chapter Five

SEMINARY YEARS AND ORDINATION, 1974-1979

MY FIRST YEAR IN THE SEMINARY I took nine philosophy courses finding some of the ideas fascinating and others utterly perplexing. I was highly motivated so I worked hard and learned a lot. I had to take it on trust that philosophy was a good foundation for studying theology. The underlying assumption was that the search for meaning (philosophy) was a corollary to the search for God (theology). I never quite understood why great philosophers like Hegel and Kant were helpful in understanding great theologians like Thomas Aquinas and Karl Rahner but I do accept that learning to think rationally is a necessary foundation in the search for God. One of the things I love about Catholicism is that it is a religion of the mind and the heart. So I persevered through courses on metaphysics (the study of being) and phenomenology (the study of consciousness) continually reminding myself that these courses were merely appetizers to the main course, the study of theology (God) and Scripture.

During that first year in the seminary, all students were required to participate in spiritual direction. I chose a priest on the faculty who preached well and had a good sense of humor as my spiritual director and I met with him every two weeks. I went into spiritual direction feeling anxious because I wasn't sure what was expected. It turned out we talked about my life in order for me to gain greater awareness of God's presence and about any obstacles that were preventing me from responding to God's presence. The spiritual director's role is that of spiritual mentor and companion on the human journey of growth and development. Good qualities I brought to our meetings were honesty and openness. I was still feeling somewhat ill-suited for priesthood because of lingering guilt over my youthful indiscretions so I decided to tell my director my life story, withholding nothing. Judging by Fr. Basso's reactions, I wasn't telling him anything new.

I learned two great lessons in spiritual direction that year: how to get in touch with my feelings, and how to trust in my own humanity. The lesson about becoming aware of my feelings happened this way: I would often complain to my spiritual director about all the problems in the world, in society, and in the seminary itself. For example, I would criticize some of my fellow seminarians for being immature and irresponsible. Dick Basso, my director, would listen to me bloviate for awhile and then ask me to pause and name how I was feeling. My eyes would look upwards, indicating I was searching for that feeling in my head. Dick would direct me to my stomach area, my gut, as the place where feelings were more likely to be found. Up to that point in my life, I'd never had much awareness of my feelings nor how feelings influenced my opinions, judgments and attitudes. Having grown up in a family which valued intellect over emotion, I believed thoughts were what mattered. I learned that year that I was carrying around a lot of anger, sadness, and fear, and that these emotions often colored my opinions and attitudes. What a revelation in self-knowledge it was to become aware of my feelings!

It was also a great gift to learn that to be a priest, I didn't need to be perfect. I gradually came to see that my past history was in no way an obstacle to becoming an effective parish priest. On the contrary, my past sins and failings were doorways to compassion and mercy for others. Dick would often counsel me to "trust my humanity" because our humanity is our meeting place with God. God's way to humans is through humans, so I began taking my own experience more seriously for therein lies the presence and action of God.

As for some of the other seminarians who appeared to me immature and irresponsible, I was right. Many of them had entered seminary in the ninth grade and now they were going through the same adolescent developmental stages that I had passed through in my teens and early twenties. Most had given up the idea of becoming priests but they stayed in the college seminary to earn their degrees. The vast majority of my fellow students at that seminary did not move on to the theological seminary the following year. In my naivete, I assumed that all seminarians would be paragons of virtue and rectitude. In fact, they were mostly fine young men in the midst of self-discovery and identity formation. I had judged some of them unfairly by forgetting my own years of immaturity and irresponsibility in high school and college. I wasn't all that mature myself but I no longer thought sitting around drinking on a weekend night was a good time.

At the end of that first year in the seminary, I felt more sure of myself and my vocation to priesthood so I enrolled in St. Patrick's Seminary in Menlo Park where I lived and studied for the next three years. The summer prior, I worked as a waiter in an upscale restaurant in Walnut Creek. My fellow waiters were intrigued by my choice of priesthood but some of them weren't so admiring of my choice to declare all my tips to the IRS. They feared that honesty on my taxes might draw the IRS' attention to their underreported earnings. I felt proud of myself for not caving in to peer pressure but my decision to declare all my tips did not win me any friends at the restaurant.

My three years at Menlo Park were wonderful and rewarding. The community of faculty, staff, and students was truly a community of friends and faith. I didn't have to feel ashamed of my faith there; everyone was committed to the same goal of priesthood in the post-Vatican II Catholic Church. Studying theology, Scripture and church history was a delight and I took full advantage of the opportunity to study and learn about the things that mattered most deeply too me. It didn't hurt that the seminary is located on a beautiful piece of land in Menlo Park that enjoys some of the best weather in the San Francisco Bay Area. Also, our meals were prepared by a group of French Canadian nuns who were terrific cooks. I still felt some trepidation about becoming a priest—still not feeling worthy—but year by year I grew into my vocation and into finding my voice.

The mid 1970's was a fairly stable time in the history of my seminary but the enrollment was relatively low compared to the pre-Vatican II era. There were about eighty students during my time there from dioceses all over the western United States with the majority coming from San Francisco and Oakland. My first year, the relative calm was shaken by the sudden departure of three priest faculty members. Their departures went largely unexplained, just a solemn announcement at Mass that Fr. X would no longer be there. Since one of the priests who left was my spiritual director, I was saddened and perplexed by his exodus. I learned later that he left in order to marry a woman with whom he had been in a relationship for years. Another priest who left had taught me Introduction to the Old Testament. I recall thinking that he seemed more admiring of Judaism than Christianity, and it turned out he left the priesthood to become a Jew. I found it peculiar that once a priest left the priesthood, his name was rarely mentioned again. The silence felt to me like a kind of shunning.

St. Patrick's Seminary has a beautiful chapel at its center and that is where the seminary community gathered for prayer services and daily Mass. The Sulpician priests--a society/organization of diocesan priests dedicated to the training of men for the parish priesthood-- who staffed the seminary were comprised of several good preachers. The liturgies were consistently nourishing with good music, full participation, and plenty of student involvement. I learned to overcome my fear of singing in large part because a close friend of mine took me and another seminarian under his wing and gave us singing lessons. The daily Masses at St. Patrick's were life-giving and inspirational. No doubt they increased my confidence about advancing toward ordination to the priesthood.

Another fond memory from my time at St. Patrick's Seminary was the friendships I developed there. Five of us formed a Jesu Caritas Fraternity (priest support group) and continued to meet monthly for many years after our ordinations to priesthood. Kevin from the Diocese of San Jose was a close friend who shared my love for learning especially mystical spirituality. He was also my tennis partner. Manny from the Diocese of Stockton and his brother George, introduced me to soccer. Ray had a room across from mine and was also from the Oakland Diocese. After ordination, we took several summer vacations together travelling around the U.S. and to Europe.

The small student body was surprisingly and refreshingly diverse: Latino, Asian, gay, straight, and an age range from twenty-five to sixty-five. Everyone embraced the reforms of Vatican II wholeheartedly.

Part of my seminary training included pastoral work outside the seminary. I did volunteer work in parishes in inner city Oakland and Newark and spent one year visiting patients at a Catholic hospital in Hayward. My work was evaluated and found acceptable. The biggest challenge I faced was teaching religion to forty fourth graders at St. Columba Parish in Oakland. On the first day of class, I asked how many of them were Catholic. When the majority didn't seem to even understand what I was asking,

I realized that most of them were either from Baptist families or of no religion at all. So I adjusted the curriculum towards a more ecumenical approach and plunged ahead in the search for God with a group of lovable kids living in inner city Oakland.

In May, 1978, I was ordained a transitional deacon and assigned to St. Leander Parish in San Leandro, just south of Oakland. The diaconate ordination is a stepping stone ritual on the path to priesthood ordination but it had my attention for its required promise of celibacy. I made the promise with trust in God and a generous willingness to sacrifice marriage and family for the sake of the Kingdom of God and the Catholic Church. I was convinced that God would supply the strength to live celibacy faithfully because that is what the Church taught. I assumed that my spiritual director who left the priesthood to marry must not have kept his guard up sufficiently.

At St. Leander, I lived in the parish rectory with five priests: the pastor, three associate pastors, and a retired priest in poor health who rarely came out of his room. The pastor was a good role model because he was personable, faith-filled, and a dynamic leader. He included me in the preaching rotation and assigned me to leading rosaries for the deceased of the parish the night before their funerals. It was an elderly parish so I spent a lot of time praying rosaries in funeral homes with grieving families. I also joined the R.C.I.A. team under the leadership of one of the associate pastors, Fr. Bob Charm. RCIA stands for Rite of Christian Initiation of Adults, the process by which adults are initiated into the Catholic faith. Bob encouraged me to read the Rite, a document of some one hundred pages, over and over until I fully understood it and internalized its vision. Another seminarian and I were put in charge of the Inquiry Period in which adults seeking baptism are encouraged to ask questions and reflect on their lives to discover the presence and action of God in their personal histories. It was an exciting and rewarding ministry that hooked me for life. The RCIA is one of the greatest innovations of Vatican II as it offers a process for adults to discover God in Scripture, community and sacraments. My work with adults seeking Christian initiation provided many of my most rewarding experiences as a priest.

I completed my deacon year at St. Leander with flying colors and was ordained a priest at St. Francis de Sales Cathedral in Oakland on June 15, 1979. I was thirty years old and embarking on the greatest adventure of my life. All of my relatives who were able attended my ordination that Friday night, and my first Mass the following day at St. Leander. I began my priestly life nervous and excited but with a great deal of support from family and friends, even the ones who were not believers. The priesthood enjoyed great respect in 1979 from Catholics and non-Catholics alike. Many of my friends and relatives felt pride in my choice of this profession.

Part II

PARISH WORK, 1979 – 2004;
WONDERS AND HORRORS

Chapter Six

OUR LADY OF THE ROSARY PARISH, UNION CITY

MY FIRST PARISH ASSIGNMENT after ordination to the priesthood, Our Lady of the Rosary (OLR), is located twenty-five miles south of Oakland in a largely Mexican and Puerto Rican neighborhood in Union City. Prior to Union City's incorporation in the late 1950's, the area was comprised of two autonomous districts: Alvarado and Decoto. Our Lady of the Rosary sits in the center of the old Decoto district. To accommodate the large numbers of Spanish speaking parishioners, the parish offered two Masses each Sunday in Spanish. I had studied Spanish in the seminary but decided to go to Cuernavaca, Mexico, for a month of Spanish studies prior to reporting for work in my new parish. I did not become fluent in a month but improved measurably. Fortunately, the two priests already assigned to the parish were fluent Spanish speakers. What I learned about Mexican culture and history was as valuable as the new vocabulary and grammar.

Growing up in foreign countries was invaluable for my adaptation to life and ministry at OLR. The people of the parish were culturally and religiously diverse and I felt welcome and useful in my role as the new associate pastor. I quickly learned the centrality of Our Lady of Guadalupe in the Mexican community when I was awoken before dawn on her feast day, Dec. 12th, by Mexican parishioners serenading us priests asleep in the rectory with joyous faith-filled songs honoring God and "la Virgen".

I noticed early on that many parishioners were very non-clerical in their religiosity. They had a strong sense of themselves as the church and many addressed priests by their first names rather than by the traditional title of "Father". I learned later that the Franciscan priests who had staffed the parish some years before had insisted on being addressed informally. The people's sense of equality with the clergy was refreshing to me and freed me from any pretensions or desire for special treatment.

There was a dynamic youth ministry team at OLR and I was assigned by the pastor to work with them in preparing and leading youth retreats. The team of young and middle aged adults taught me the importance of taking teenagers seriously and encouraging them to use their talents for building up the community of faith.

The printed materials we used for many of our retreat skits and educational games had been written by my predecessor at O.L.R., a priest named Steve Kiesle. I had never met Steve because he'd been removed from active ministry for sexually abusing at least two boys at O.L.R. Steve wasn't talked about much by the youth ministry team or the other parishioners but what little I did learn was that he was generally well liked, very gifted at youth ministry, but that his work was undermined by his alcoholism. His sexual crimes against boys in the parish were so unspeakably horrible to everyone in the parish that little was spoken of them. The silence about the topic of Fr. Steve's fall from grace was indicative of people close to Fr. Steve feeling betrayed by him. But the silence also manifested a taboo associated with priests' sexuality. Priests were not generally viewed as men with sexual feelings and desires. For the people of OLR to learn that Fr. Steve sexually molested two boys in the parish indicated that he was not only a sexual being but a very disturbed one. The silence indicated the taboo nature of the topic and mirrored the secrecy and silence of Church authorities around the topic of priests and sex, especially criminal sex.

One day, less than a year before my arrival at OLR, Steve was arrested and taken away. Steve Kiesle's name and misdeeds would resurface repeatedly in the ensuing years. The year 1979 was a long time before the Boston Globe blew the roof off the Catholic Church in 2002 with its landmark series on widespread clergy sexual abuse. I was shaken when I learned of Steve's crimes and could not imagine how and why a priest would sexually abuse youth. I felt great sympathy for friends of Steve in the parish who were quietly struggling to understand this tragedy. I understood the abuse as an anomaly, crimes perpetrated by a disturbed human being who happened to be a priest. At the time, I didn't see Steve's crimes as having anything to do with the priesthood; it was simply a case of one bad apple in a big barrel full of good priests, faithful to their promises.

My life at OLR was enjoyable, rewarding and challenging. I learned much about how to celebrate Mass in English and Spanish, how to conduct baptisms, weddings, and anointings of the sick. I learned the importance of youth ministry and something of the challenge of unifying an ethnically diverse parish with services in two languages. I learned about accompanying people through tragedy and heartbreak. My first summer at OLR, I presided at three funerals of young people: victims of accidents and a murder. I learned that at times there is nothing to say to take the pain away, and that just being present with compassion is the best gift one has to offer. I learned how much a priest's ministry is appreciated and valued and how hard it is to leave a community in which I had been so immersed and appreciated.

Chapter Seven

ST. BEDE PARISH, HAYWARD

TWO YEARS INTO MY THREE YEAR ASSIGNMENT at OLR, I got a call from an official at the Diocese asking me to transfer to St. Bede Parish in Hayward where Msgr. George Francis had been pastor since founding the parish in the mid 1950's. I would have preferred to stay at OLR at least one more year but did not see how I could say no to the Bishop's representative. My training and temperament resulted in a submissive attitude toward Church authority so I assumed that I was being transferred prematurely for good reason.

The reason, which I only learned about much later, was that I was being transferred at the request of Msgr. George Francis whose two associate pastors were barely on speaking terms. George had attended a priests' retreat Mass at which I presided. He was sufficiently impressed that he asked the Bishop, John Cummins, to have me transferred to St. Bede. So I moved there in 1981 with some trepidation knowing of George's reputation as a very traditional and strict pastor whose assistant priests did not stay long. Bishop Cummins acceded to George's request because the Monsignor was a prodigious fundraiser.

St. Bede is located in a working class neighborhood in south Hayward. The ethnic diversity of the area was reflected in the parish's offering of Mass in Spanish. The street where the parish church and school was located also hosted several other churches, some convalescent homes, and several low rent apartment complexes.

St. Bede was a large parish with over three hundred infant baptisms a year, five Masses a weekend, and many funerals and weddings. Since I was sent there to replace two priests, I knew I would be busy, and indeed I was. I worked extremely hard and felt welcome and appreciated from the beginning by the parishioners. The biggest change affecting me was that in addition to a lot more work, the pastor was generally disliked except for a small clique of parishioners who formed his inner circle. George Francis' three main interests were the parish school, CYO boys basketball, and raising money. He alienated many people with his repeated appeals for money and with his gruff and strict way of dealing with people who came to him with their problems. George was always obliging towards me but I think I annoyed him with my repeated efforts to update the liturgy according to the standards of Vatican II liturgical reforms. For example, I worked for months to convince George to allow Communion from the cup at all the Masses. He initially opposed this change because he thought it would cause a logistical nightmare viz a viz the distribution of Holy Communion, and that it would cost too much money to provide so much wine each weekend. Gradually I won him over to the change by assuring him how well Communion under both species (bread and wine) worked smoothly in other parishes, and how the cost of wine would not be prohibitive.

Another example of George's rigid traditionalism would have Martin Luther turning over in his grave. On All Souls Day (Nov. 2nd) each year, George would schedule each priest to preside at three Masses, one every twenty minutes. My first All Souls Day in the parish, there were three priests assigned to the parish plus a hospital chaplain in residence. That meant there were twelve Masses scheduled in one day to commemorate the "souls

in purgatory". I asked George why so many Masses were necessary and he explained that the Church allowed for three Masses
per priest that day, a rule he considered a great privilege. In fact,
the more Masses offered made it easier to justify the money of-
ferings/stipends that the parishioners were donating in memory
of their beloved deceased family and friends. These stipends went
directly to the priests as additional income. We priests typically
received around one thousand dollars from stipends for that one
day. A priest friend of mine called All Souls Day "clergy Christmas". I was scandalized by this practice and let George know I
didn't think it was right, and to please schedule me in the future
for just one Mass on All Souls Day. George and I were living in
two different theological universes but he usually gave in to my
requests if I persisted.

After my first couple of Holy Weeks at St. Bede, I suggested
to George that we change the Good Friday liturgy in accord
with liturgical reforms. He responded: "Why would we change
it? We've always done it that way." I patiently explained that the
people taking the trouble to attend Good Friday services might
be bored by three hours of sermonizing, and that the simple
three part liturgy called for by the Church would more than
satisfy their spiritual needs. I may as well have been speaking
Greek to him, a man who never read a book or paid attention
to liturgical reforms.

I learned to pick my battles carefully with George but I found
over time that my levels of anger and frustration were growing
steadily. I lasted four years in that assignment in part because I felt
devoted to the people and in part because two priests were suc-
cessively assigned there whom I liked and enjoyed working with.
They provided more community in the house and more support
in implementing the reforms of Vatican II.

But those two priests eventually were reassigned and life
in that rectory grew very lonely for me. The hospital chaplain

in residence was an alcoholic who drank to inebriation every evening. The other associate pastor was an arrogant man whose foreign accent was hard for the people to understand, and who looked down on the Latino parishioners. I vividly recall dinners in the rectory where I felt constrained from talking about anything other than sports or the weather lest I upset George or create tension between him and the alcoholic priest. There was no love loss between the two of them.

In spite of the fact that working with George Francis was frustrating and challenging for me, I did learn enough about him to sometimes feel sorry for him. When I arrived at St. Bede, George was in his early seventies, had been a priest for over fifty years, and had entered the seminary in the ninth grade. He told me he had followed his brother into the seminary but that his brother had not been ordained. I asked George why he stayed and got ordained. He told me he didn't know what else to do with his life. I could tell that he was emotionally immature and related more easily to children than to adults. He found a lot of joy and satisfaction in coaching CYO boys basketball teams. He also would spend a lot of time at the parish school and kept school tuition artificially low to make it easier on parents to keep their children in the school. So at times I felt sorry for George but more so for the many parishioners he hurt by his gruff demeanor and often black and white advice. His obsession with fund raising was embarrassing to watch as he alienated many parishioners by his manipulative and constant appeals to their generosity using guilt, arm twisting, and shaming to increase the Sunday collection.

The alienation I experienced in the rectory coupled with the heavy workload of a large parish gradually lowered my morale and happiness. I enjoyed the support of a priest support group which met monthly, a spiritual director, a supportive family, and friends outside the parish but I found myself being drawn into problematic situations with a few women parishioners. I was strongly tempted to cross the boundaries imposed by mandatory celibacy to assuage my need for intimacy and sexual contact. I will write more about the dynamics of sexuality for a priest committed to celibacy in the chapter on "Mandatory Celibacy". My situation became so problematic that I sought out counseling toward the goal of asking for a transfer to another parish. In the summer of 1985, bowed but not broken, I transferred to St. John Vianney Parish in Walnut Creek. The Diocese initially asked me to go to a parish with a pastor similar in temperament to Msgr. Francis but I stood my ground and insisted on a better living situation. The counseling helped me to speak up for myself and my needs. Though my new parish was far away from St. Bede's in Hayward, I had not heard the last of George Francis who, it turned out, was a serial pedophile. Unbeknownst to me, he was sexually abusing a little girl during my stay at St. Bede. I will elaborate further in chapter twenty-two on Clergy Sexual Abuse.

Chapter Eight

ST. JOHN VIANNEY PARISH, WALNUT CREEK

ST. JOHN VIANNEY IS THE PATRON SAINT of parish priests which I interpreted as a good omen for my new assignment. Walnut Creek is an affluent city in Contra Costa County, about twenty miles northeast of Oakland. The parish was founded in the 1950's to accommodate suburban growth and a post World War II population boom. The parish, which we called SJV for short, was known around town as "the country club on the hill" because of its many affluent and well-dressed parishioners and its location on a small hill overlooking the Diablo Valley. Mt. Diablo, one of the taller mountains in the Bay Area, sits majestically overlooking Walnut Creek and the surrounding area.

The pastor and associate pastor were close friends with each other and they welcomed me warmly. Manny and Tom were a breath of fresh air after four years of rectory life with Msgr. George Francis. Tom was from Louisiana and liked to cook Cajun recipes from time to time. Manny, a gentle and kind man, pastored the parish with love. The parish staff included several women who were competent in their ministries and who the pastor treated as equals.

At first I felt a little intimidated by the high education levels of many parishioners especially in terms of my preaching to them, but that feeling didn't last long. The people appreciated my preaching and teaching and welcomed me warmly. SJV provided a place to heal and rejuvenate after the four years of struggle and disillusionment at St. Bede. I missed the ethnic diversity of my first two assignments and the greater sense of feeling needed that I experienced in those two blue collar parishes, but the happier rectory life more than compensated.

During my four year assignment at SJV, Pope John Paul II visited San Francisco and celebrated a memorable Mass at Candlestick Park. I joined a busload of parishioners to attend that event and felt honored to be a eucharistic minister (distributor of Communion) to a section of people in the upper deck. The Pope made a very positive impression on me by the way he greeted the capacity crowd upon his entrance to the stadium to begin Mass and by the devotion with which he presided at the Mass. The Bay Area fell in love with the Polish pope for his warmth and compassion. I felt proud to be a Catholic and a priest.

During those days in Walnut Creek, the shortage of priests in the United States and many other countries was becoming a growing concern. I took part in various efforts to attract more young men to the priesthood and joined a committee to promote the priesthood in colleges and high schools. Our efforts were mixed at best and the shortage worsened.

Although I enjoyed my work in the parish and experienced warmth and belonging in the rectory and beyond, I still felt a longing for female companionship and emotional and sexual intimacy. By this time I was in my mid thirties and had been mostly celibate since age 24. I had committed to a celibate life knowingly and willingly but as time passed, the absence of intimacy grew more painful. I would at times feel incomplete and look upon married couples in the parish with envy. I coped with these feelings through prayer, exercise, my priest support group, and group counseling. I never discussed my struggles with the priests in the rectory nor did they share their struggles with me. Any sexual activity by priests, including masturbation, was deemed sinful by Church teaching, an atmosphere which engendered shame, guilt, and secrecy. I was a diocesan priest, as opposed to a religious one belonging to a religious order such as the Jesuits and Franciscans. Religious order priests live in communities where in theory they enjoy emotional support and friendship where they live, whereas diocesan priests typically live in a rectory, sometimes alone or with another priest or two. Diocesan priests do not get to choose the priests with whom they live. Often there is little or no expectation of community in diocesan parish rectories. I continued to believe in a celibate priesthood out of tradition and practicality but in my heart I experienced loneliness and longing.

After four years at St. John Vianney, I was asked to consider becoming a pastor (priest in charge) but I told my representative on the Diocese's Personnel Board that I did not feel ready for such a responsibility. Thankfully, my request was respected and I was reassigned as an associate pastor to St. Raymond Parish in Dublin.

Chapter Nine

ST. RAYMOND PARISH, DUBLIN

DURING THE TIME I SPENT IN DUBLIN, 1989-1992, it was a small suburban city southeast of the Oakland hills, located in the heart of the Tri-valley area (Dublin, Pleasanton, Livermore). Its name hearkens back to its early settlers of Irish American descent. St. Raymond Parish is predominantly middle class and Caucasian but had a growing number of Filipinos and Latinos.

The pastor of St. Raymond Parish, Dick Matgen, welcomed me warmly. We were the same age and both avid San Francisco Giants fans. He was a good preacher and an excellent administrator. I considered him a friend and confidante. He confided in me early on that he was gay, a courageous sign of transparency. I knew of gay priests but not any who dared to admit it. In reply, I thanked him for his trust in me. Dick's openness created an atmosphere of trust and honesty and paved the way for friendship and collaboration in ministry.

Our parish staff was comprised of six women, the pastor, and myself. The predominance of women reflected the fact that women far outnumber men in doing the day to day work of professional ministry. How ironic and sad then that women are excluded from pastoring parishes and dioceses in the Catholic Church's leadership structure.

One of the most exciting and rewarding aspects of our staff interaction was the amount of time and energy we invested in community building as a staff. At one of our annual staff retreats, we hired a facilitator to help us in communicating with one another, a process which involved listening skills and a willingness to acknowledge emotional dissonance when it surfaced. Our care for one another as staff members had a positive impact on the ministries and services for and with the people of the parish.

Although I was fully engaged in my work at St. Raymond, preaching, teaching, social justice ministry and community building, I knew that sooner than later I would be asked by the Diocese to pastor a parish. The shortage of priests was becoming more acute and by 1989 when I arrived at St. Raymond, I had been ordained a priest for ten years. Soon enough, in 1992, I was asked by the Bishop, via a member of the priest Personnel Board, to transfer to St. Benedict Parish in east Oakland as pastor. A visit there along with a little research revealed St. Benedict Parish to be poor and located in a very depressed neighborhood riddled with drugs and crime. I had often taught and preached the need to serve the poor, and here was a chance for me to put my words into practice. I told the Personnel Board member that I was willing to be pastor of St. Benedict. However, before the transfer could be finalized, I was contacted and asked instead to be pastor at Corpus Christi Parish in Fremont. I inquired why the change in plans and was told that a crisis had arisen at Corpus Christi that required a bilingual pastor (English and Spanish) and that I was viewed as the best fit for the position. Since I had been wanting to get back to using my Spanish and had some familiarity with that area of the Diocese, I agreed to accept the appointment.

Chapter Ten

CORPUS CHRISTI PARISH, FREMONT

AFTER A WARM SEND-OFF FROM ST. RAYMOND, I moved into Corpus Christi the day before Thanksgiving, 1992. I remember feeling both confident and insecure as a new pastor. The confidence derived from all I had learned working with Father Dick Matgen and the rest of the staff at St. Raymond as well as my years of pastoral experience and preaching at four different parishes over a thirteen year period. The insecurity arose in part from my fear of responsibility—being pastor is a much greater responsibility than being associate pastor—and my experiential knowledge of how challenging it is to be a competent pastor. Friends reminded me that I would have lots of help from parishioners and staff, and that I had more than enough talent and faith to succeed in the job. One wise friend counseled me to view problems as opportunities. So what better day to celebrate the first Eucharist with my new community than Thanksgiving!

As I mentioned earlier, I was sent to Corpus Christi in the wake of a crisis involving the removal of the Franciscan priest, Fr. Rigo, who had been ministering to the Latino members of the parish by the pastor, Fr. Dunn, who had held the position for six years. The Latino community, who comprised forty percent of the parish, was upset with the Diocese for not reinstating Fr. Rigo, after he'd been dismissed by Fr. Dunn. Latino leaders had picketed the church during Sunday masses to protest Fr. Rigo's dismissal. Their public demonstration came to the Bishop's attention motivating him to send a mediator to the parish to resolve the crisis. Ultimately, the Diocese decided to transfer the pastor and replace him and Fr. Rigo with me.

I spent my first few months in the parish listening to anyone willing to talk to me about what had transpired during the crisis including visits with Fathers Dunn and Rigo. Most of those who wanted to talk about it felt Fr. Rigo had been treated unjustly. He was obviously well loved so to see him summarily dismissed by the pastor was a terrible shock to many. I listened and listened and gradually the people accepted the new arrangement. In the meantime, I jumped with both feet into the ministry of the parish: Masses in both Spanish and English, baptisms, funerals, weddings, and administration of the finances and buildings.

Although my knowledge of Spanish was far from fluent, the Latino community was welcoming and appreciative of my efforts even when I felt I was making a fool of myself. Sometimes during a homily or talk in Spanish, I would be at a loss for a particular word and ask out loud, "como se dice en espanol?" ("How do you say it in Spanish?"). Even if my talk was less than stellar, the people felt engaged by my need for and openness to tutoring. It didn't take me long to feel at home in the parish but I faced some major challenges: a parish debt, a need to eliminate one weekend Mass, and the need for a pastoral plan (goal setting and visioning). I will elaborate further on these challenges later on. To my advantage, I had time on my side since a pastor's term is six years renewable for six more years. I had help from the Pastoral Council and Finance Council I inherited from Fr. Dunn. I had faith in God, a comfortable rectory, a charming neighborhood, a youth minister/religious education director, a parish secretary, and a gardener/handyman. At times when a decision had to be made, it took getting used to the fact that as pastor, the buck stopped with me. Yes, me! I kept reminding myself that the worst

I could do was fail, but that if I was lucky, I might just grow up and into my new responsibilities. Priests do not enjoy the three circumstances most likely to prompt maturity in American men: a wife, children, and the struggle to make a living. But becoming pastor of a parish has its own circumstances for inviting a priest to grow up so I will now highlight several of those circumstances.

Chapter Eleven

THE PARISH DEBT

FOR READERS UNFAMILIAR WITH Church funding sources, parishes are funded by the parishioners' donations to the Sunday Mass collections. Parishes are required to give a percentage of their income to the diocese which the diocese uses to pay its bills and help out poorer parishes. Corpus Christi was self-sustaining but had fallen behind on its payments to the Diocese.

Fr. Dunn, my predecessor as pastor, had inherited from his predecessor a cash surplus in 1986 and left six years later with a parish debt of $140,000, a substantial figure for a small parish. The Diocese asked me to arrange for an independent audit to respond to rumors of financial impropriety from parishioners. Fortunately, the audit accounted for all the funds but we still faced the challenge of a significant debt. The parish secretary/bookkeeper agonized over which bills to delay paying each month. I noticed right away that the small parish staff was underpaid and that there was a huge discrepancy between the male gardener's salary and the two female staff members' salaries. The gardener made $10,000 more a year.

I had barely heard of the concept of stewardship at that time but I knew I had to quickly let the parishioners know the state of the parish finances and invite them to take ownership. The very thought of talking about money during Mass caused me trepidation because of painful memories of Msgr. George Francis talking about money incessantly. He used to insist that everyone donate each Sunday using parish offertory envelopes and "everyone" included children. I used to cringe with embarrassment as Monsignor would use guilt and shame to manipulate and emotionally coerce people into donating to the parish. In light of those memories, I dreaded having to ask the people of Corpus Christi for increased giving.

I talked the situation over with the parish finance committee who were a great help in formulating a plan to get the parish back onto a solid financial footing. Committee members comprised three to five volunteers with skills in financial management. I also talked it over with a close priest friend of mine. When I told him how I dreaded talking to the parishioners about the need for more money, he asked me how much I was donating to the Sunday collection. I said that I didn't donate anything because the parish was paying my salary. He failed to see my logic and told me I shouldn't ask the people to give if I wasn't willing to, and he made things worse by declaring that I should be giving 5% of my salary to the parish and 5% to the poor, all in the Jewish and Christian tradition of the tithe. I was getting a crash course in stewardship wherein all we have is a gift from God to be shared generously with others. So I signed up for parish envelopes and let the people know I would be donating 5% of my salary to the parish from then on. The response was overwhelmingly positive. Collections increased along with individual gifts for particular needs. Within six years, we were out of debt and able to meet our financial obligations. Gradually we were able to increase all the salaries of the staff and to equalize the male and female salaries.

In the meantime, we learned that someone had named Corpus Christi in their will and that the parish would be receiving some money upon the death of that person's heir. No one in the parish knew the donor nor his heir whose identity was not revealed. I assumed one of my successors would be the pastor when the inheritance became available. To my delight, sometime around 2000, the parish received a check for $160,000. I was overjoyed and amazed at God's generosity. Not forgetting what we'd just learned about stewardship, we donated 10% of that gift to charity. Stewardship really works!

My experience in financial administration had a happy ending. I was grateful for the valuable help of the finance committee and the generosity of the people. Finance committees are mandated in every parish by Canon Law but pastors and bishops still remain too unaccountable for their stewardship of people's donations. The journalist and author Jason Berry's 2011 book, REN-DER UNTO ROME—THE SECRET LIFE OF MONEY IN THE CATHOLIC CHURCH, exposes the large amount of corruption, greed, and dishonesty in the use and abuse of money by clergy from the Vatican to the dioceses to the parishes. People too readily assume and trust that clergy will practice responsible stewardship with donated money but the truth of the matter is that there is a lot of theft happening at every level of the Church. Finance committees have access to the books but that assumes that the books reflect the truth of income and expenses. Financial transparency and accountability will not happen until clerical control of money is relinquished and a more transparent system adopted. I had no training in financial administration and learned by the seat of my pants. In retrospect, I think that responsibility for finances should be taken completely out of the hands of the priests and bishops to free them up for preaching, teaching and community building.

Chapter Twelve

CHANGING THE MASS SCHEDULE AND DEVISING A PLAN FOR PARISH RENEWAL

ONE OF THE CHALLENGES I FACED early on was to change the Mass schedule by eliminating one Mass from the five weekend Mass schedule. Five Masses were not needed, given low attendance, and I needed to have a manageable workload. Everyone agreed we didn't need five Masses each weekend but no one wanted "their" Mass eliminated. A curious fact of parish life is that because most Catholics attend the same Mass each weekend, that Mass becomes their reference point and community in the parish. To ask people to attend another Mass means more than just a time change in their weekend routine.

I consulted with parish leaders and we decided to start with a survey offering different Mass schedules for their consideration. Many interpreted the survey as an election which led to some anger when we'd settled on a new Mass schedule. Several people switched parishes once the new schedule was implemented. The whole process was painful and awkward. Years later we had to change the Mass schedule again to accommodate a Sunday Mass at 6 p.m. That time there was less controversy because the change was meant to accommodate the youth of the parish.

Once the finances were stabilized and I had gotten to know a large number of parishioners, the Pastoral Council (twelve parish leaders) and I began a discernment process for elucidating goals and objectives for the parish. We agreed that the key to an alive and dynamic parish was not good programs but virbrant community characterized by love and concern among parishioners. I recalled that during my deacon year of 1978-1979, I had participated in a Cursillo weekend. Cursillo means literally "little course" in Spanish. Cursillo was started by a priest in Spain to foster deeper spirituality among the laity. Later, Cursillos caught fire in the United States including in the Diocese of Oakland. During my own Cursillo weekend in 1979, I experienced church as community for the first time in my life. A key component of the Cursillo experience is faith-sharing within a small group, which means relating faith to daily life. Faith-sharing is not about religion per se but about one's experience of God in the events and people of daily life. Cursillo encourages all who have made the weekend to join a Cursillo support group for ongoing growth in piety, study and action. While at St. John Vianney, I belonged to such a group but always lamented the fact that Cursillo was not more integrated into the life of the parish. I wanted to discover a way for every parishioner to belong to a small faith community comprised of fellow parishioners. Cursillo support groups are typically comprised of people from many parishes who typically do not worship together nor spend much time together outside of their monthly reunions. The challenge for us as a Council was how to foster and support dynamic community building among parishioners of the same passion and effectiveness as the Cursillo movement.

The Diocese at that time was considering adopting RENEW, a national faith renewal program, but a final decision kept being put off by the bishop. In the meantime, I happened upon a book by Fr. Art Baranowski of the Archdiocese of Detroit called RESTRUCTURING THE PARISH INTO SMALL FAITH COMMUNITIIES. Reading that book was a revelation for me because it provided a pastoral model and plan for how to make small faith communities a new and more personal means of experiencing church within a parish and diocese. The key aspect of Baranowski's plan was faith-sharing, people connecting faith with daily life on a weekly or biweekly basis with 8 to 12 other parishioners. Faith-sharing is not primarily talk about religion; faith-sharing is primarily talking about one's experience of God in daily life. God after all comes to humans through humans and is present in goodness, beauty, and truth, as well as in experiences of hardship, grief, and alienation. Art's book wasn't just theoretical; he succeeded in restructuring his own Detroit parish into thirty-four small faith communities. He in turn was convincing other pastors in the Detroit area to restructure their parishes too.

After reading that book, I could hardly contain my enthusiasm. I bought copies for all the Pastoral Council members, the parish staff, and other key leaders in the parish. I thought to myself, here is a pastoral plan that's workable, that has the potential to revolutionize people's faith, and to build community like Cursillo does, but rooted in the parish with the same people one worships with every Sunday. I had had an epiphany and couldn't wait to share my treasure with others.

At about the same time the Pastoral Council had agreed to adopting Baranowski's pastoral plan, the Diocese finally adopted RENEW as its own pastoral plan for every parish. RENEW is a three year process which brings parishioners together periodically to connect faith to daily life via small groups. At Corpus Christi, we decided to use RENEW groups as an introduction to creating permanent small faith communities.

After many years of hard work, the parish ended up with 8 small church communities. We called them church communities instead of faith communities because of Baranowski's insistence that these communities are really church at a more personal level. He delineated four levels of church: universal (with headquarters at the Vatican), diocese, parish, and small church. Each small church of 8 to 12 members had a trained pastoral facilitator (PF). I would meet with all the PF's every two months for support and ongoing formation. The small churches generally met every two weeks for fellowship, prayer, and faith sharing.

Reflecting back on our experience of parish restructuring, it's clear that only a small percentage of parishioners were ever involved. Convincing a Catholic to join a small church community (SCC) is a hard sell. It requires a time commitment of two hours twice a month which is a challenge for many busy people. Joining a SCC is also a new way of doing/being church for people who have not made a Cursillo or been part of a small group that involves faith-sharing. Most Catholics equate faith with beliefs learned in catechism/CCD or parochial school. But faith-sharing in a SCC is more about recognizing God's presence in one's life and sharing that experience with fellow small church members. Faith-sharing requires that one take his or her life experience seriously because that is where we experience God's presence and action. Faith sharing also requires a person to reflect on their daily life in order to deepen awareness of God's presence. Faith-sharing is thus countercultural in that it asks people to slow down, reflect, and trust that God is present in the myriad events of daily life.

Another challenge for small churches is the recruiting, training, and supporting of pastoral facilitators. PF's function as pastors and pastoring is not easy. A good pastor needs to be a good listener, patient, kind, with respect for diversity and the courage to deal with conflict directly and wisely. He or she also needs to have an interior life and some self-awareness. The competent pastor facilitates with a light but confident touch.

I left Corpus Christi in 2004. Today, ten years later, there are two small churches that continue to meet. Their PF's no longer meet with the pastor of the parish. When Fr. Art Baranowski was moved from his restructured parish in Detroit, there were 34 small churches. Art's successor did not share Art's vision of church and never supported the small churches or their PF's. Eventually, those 34 small churches began to dwindle and disband. I once asked Art how he dealt with that sad news and he admitted it was hard to see his best efforts end in futility but that he intended to start anew in his next parish assignment. All of this begs the question: what does it mean to be church? But before I address that question, let me recount how and why we addressed another goal, outreach to youth.

Chapter Thirteen

TAKING YOUTH SERIOUSLY

THE PASTORAL PLAN TO RESTRUCTURE THE PARISH into small church communities of 8 to 12 members headed by a pastoral facilitator did not address directly parishioners' concern for more outreach to teenagers of the parish. Whenever Catholics are asked to list their concerns, very often their top priority is the youth. How can the parish help teenagers find meaning and joy through more active participation in the life of the parish?

Providentially, a priest friend of mine had recently started a Life Teen Mass at his parish in San Jose. Life Teen is a Catholic teen program started in the Phoenix area in the 1980's. Life Teen spread like wild fire to other parts of the U.S. and throughout the English speaking world. Its great innovation was to build a parish teen program around a Sunday evening Mass geared for teenagers in which the teens are actively involved in many facets of the Mass. Teens lector, help distribute Communion, take up the collection, gather around the altar for the Eucharistic Prayer, and greet people as they arrive and depart the service. The music is played and sung in a rock style with guitars, drums, and piano. After Mass, the teens gather for Life Night which at our parish comprised a meal, socializing, service and faith formation.

I was curious enough in my friend Fr. Kevin Joyce's Life Teen Mass in San Jose that I, along with Lucy Soltau, our youth minister, went to check it out. We both loved the experience and set about planning how we could start a Life Teen Mass at Corpus Christi, Fremont. The two biggest hurdles were changing the Mass schedule to accommodate a 6 p.m. Sunday Mass, and creating a band to offer liturgical music and song in rock style. Lucy is an accomplished guitarist and singer so she generously agreed to form a band and lead it every Sunday evening. Seemingly out of nowhere came two other guitarists, a drummer, a keyboardist, and a percussionist. Changing the Mass schedule again after the divisiveness caused by our earlier schedule change went much smoother than I imagined. We eliminated the 12:30 p.m. Mass with its sparse attendance to make room for a 6 p.m. Mass. Teens would no longer be able to complain of having to get up early on Sunday for Mass.

The Life Teen Mass also required a Core Team to be formed to plan the Mass each week. Lucy and I were permanent Core Team members along with four volunteers. One of our weekly tasks was to create a skit which took place just after the Scripture readings and just before the homily. The skit was designed to express a theme or lesson from the readings and these skits turned out to be one of the most popular features of the Mass.

The Life Teen Mass was not only popular with teenagers but also with their younger brothers and sisters, parents, grandparents, friends and neighbors. And it was popular with me because it increased my faith and the faith of many in attendance.

The Life Teen movement nationally has stalled somewhat due to the arrest of its dynamic priest founder for sexual involvement with teens at St. Timothy's Parish in Mesa, Arizona. Subsequently, another pastor of St. Timothy's has also been removed from ministry for sexual abuse of youth. In spite of those setbacks, the Life Teen model for youth ministry works well at Corpus Christi and proved to be one of my most rewarding efforts. Teenagers have much to offer a parish through their vitality and talents and Corpus Christi experienced that first-hand and continues to offer Life Teen today.

In spite of the success of the youth Mass and our efforts to establish small church communities, I was beginning to feel isolated from the Diocese and the larger Catholic Church world both in my diocese and beyond. I began to experience feelings of disillusionment and futility based on my unsuccessful efforts to get the Oakland Diocese to address problems facing the universal Church and the Church throughout the United States.

Chapter Fourteen

WHAT DOES IT MEAN TO BE CHURCH?

THIS IS NOT AN ABSTRACT QUESTION. Jesus did not leave a blueprint for how to organize the Church but in the Gospels he has much to say about how authority should be exercised and how his followers must love one another if they are to mirror God's love. For the rest, Jesus left it up to his followers to decide under the guidance of the Holy Spirit how the church would be structured.

In the seminary, all candidates for priesthood take a course entitled "Ecclesiology", the study of church. My priest professor, Father Mo Duchaine, asked us on the first day of class to define church. We students came up with a long and diverse list of definitions, but I think what Mo was really doing was stressing the importance of asking the question, "what is the church?", and to keep on asking it the rest of our lives. There is no one answer to this critically important question. The ancient creeds list the four marks of the church as "one, holy, catholic, and apostolic". The Vatican II document on the Church has several descriptions of church including: people of God, sacrament, mystery and institution.

Church isn't a place but rather a way of being together characterized by faith, hope, and love that leads to ministry/service and witness to Jesus and the Gospel. For the majority of Catholics in the United States, attending Mass on Sunday is their only experience of church week to week. Although a good liturgy strives to get everyone involved through full, conscious and active participation, I became convinced that small churches are essential to mature faith and discipleship. The Church teaches that mature faith includes an experiential loving knowledge of God through Jesus in the Holy Spirit. In our culture where business, busyness, and distraction are the norm for most people, I believe that small churches provide an experience of attention to God in oneself, in others, and in daily life, and that a lived experience of God who is love is transformative.

I used to teach parishioners that before we could "do" church, we had to "be" church. At the beginning of every meeting no matter its agenda, I would ask people to check in briefly with each other about how they were doing and feeling. That way, people felt more connected to each other which in turn led to more productive work.

The sheer size of most Catholic parishes mitigates against people growing in personal presence, prayer, reflection, and awareness of God in self and others. One of the blessings of being pastor of Corpus Christi is that it is a relatively small parish of about 800 families with a Sunday Mass attendance of under 1,000. Larger parishes, even with the best of leadership and intentions, often become Mass factories where the chances of getting familiar with God and fellow parishioners are slim. Many people at Corpus Christi knew each other well both from fellowship in the parish but also from the surrounding neighborhoods, schools, civic and sports programs.

So although the small size of the parish was conducive to church as a community of faith and friendship, we had several barriers to that kind of church: individualism, clericalism, and the absence of women in the priesthood. Much has been written about individualism in our culture. I will revisit the problem of clericalism and the exclusion of women in later chapters.

I mentioned earlier the guidance of the Holy Spirit for the creation and development of church structures in keeping with Gospel values. The earliest communities of Christian believers had a strong awareness of the Spirit's role in their growth and development. Church governance and structure is secondary to the presence of the Holy Spirit in believers drawing us all toward unity in love and justice. Early believers relied on the Spirit for guidance and strength as emphasized in the Acts of the Apostles. Other books of the New Testament reflect different emphases in church organization (see Raymond Brown's THE CHURCHES THE APOSTLES LEFT BEHIND (Paulist Press, 1984). Jesus promised that the church would never fail precisely because of the Holy Spirit's presence and guidance. When church leaders and members forget or lose awareness of the Spirit, church life atrophies and dies through boredom, routine, and stagnation. No one person or group in the church has a monopoly of the Spirit. All believers share in the Spirit by baptism and confirmation. The church is not the structure, the doctrine, the buildings, or the hierarchy, though all of these are important aspects of church life; the church is the living community of faith, animated and directed by the Holy Spirit of the risen Christ. In the following chapters, I will relate various experiences which gradually revealed to me an institutional church in dire need of structural reform in order for the Holy Spirit to breathe freely into the hearts and minds of believers. Fr. Mo Duchaine's probing question is as relevant as ever.

Chapter Fifteen

THE PERSONNEL BOARD OR MISSION IMPOSSIBLE

BY THE LATE 1980's THE PRIEST SHORTAGE was becoming acute and I began advocating for addressing this crisis which was affecting the morale of priests and the quality of priest leadership in the parishes. I did so by bringing it up in every forum available including letters to the Bishop and the Diocese's newspaper, the Priests Senate and Personnel Board. Due to my outspokenness and persistence, my peers elected me to serve a four year term on the Priest Personnel Board in the mid 1990's. A priest who had already served on the Board told me that Board meetings were extremely painful to endure. I was about to find out what he meant.

The Personnel Board met about ten times a year to make recommendations to the Bishop about which priests to assign to which parishes. There were roughly ten members, some elected and some ex officio members. When I joined the Board, all members were priests save for one woman who was the ethnic ministries director. Later during my tenure, the Board membership was expanded to include lay people appointed by the Bishop. The Board's authority is strictly advisory. The bishop of Oakland at that time was John Cummins and he had ultimate authority over assignments. His practice was to show up to our meetings towards the end to receive our recommendations. Thus, he did not take part in our deliberations.

The deliberations customarily followed a pattern: the priest Personnel Director/Vicar for Clergy would inform us about positions needing to be filled. For example, he might inform us that the pastor of parish X had died and thus needed replacing, and that the parochial vicar (associate pastor) at parish Y was due for a transfer and thus needed replacing. On a blackboard would be listed the names of priests available for assignment or due for reassignment. These were priests typically completing their terms as pastors and parochial vicars, or priests returning from sabbatical or sick leave. Occasionally we had newly ordained priests to assign.

At some point during my time on the Board, we started sending two Board members to parishes in need of a new pastor to hear from parishioners the kind of pastor they thought the parish needed, e.g. Spanish speaking, good administrator, or competent preacher.

What made my experience of Board meetings so painful was that the shortage of priests limited the Board's ability to make good assignments, or sometimes any assignment at all. Large parishes that had once had three priests were being reduced to two; medium size parishes with two priests were being reduced to one; small parishes with one priest were being considered for consolidation or closure. The priest shortage was acute and not just in terms of quantity; quality was also a big problem. Some priests lacked people skills, others were poor preachers or administrators. Others were known to be lazy or angry or non-collaborative. Some foreign priests were hard to understand. Some priests refused to be transferred; others had been told they could never be pastors.

Surveys indicate that the biggest single influence on the success of a parish is the pastor. Knowing this, I took my responsibility to assign competent priests as pastors very seriously. But more often than not, there was no competent priest to assign as pastor because all the competent ones were already assigned. It occurred to me early on that we needed to expand the pool of priests available to pastor parishes, and that the wisest way to do so would be to allow priests to marry and to ordain women. Knowing the controversial nature of these two ideas, I raised the issue to my fellow Board members thusly: we have a serious obligation to make quality assignments of priests to parishes; month after month we find ourselves agonizing over whom to assign and often feel dissatisfied with our choices (I often voted against the majority because I refused to assign a priest whom I knew to be incompetent or problematic). Does it not make sense for us to begin studying how we can expand the pool of priests to ensure that every parish has competent priests?

What kind of reaction do you suppose I received? The typical response was to the effect that Board members did not have the authority to decide on who is eligible for ordination so it would be a waste of our valuable time to discuss the topic. Then the subject would be changed. I would sometimes counter that it was irresponsible for us to assign priests lacking the talents needed to be competent pastors and parochial vicars. Then I'd be told I was being too judgmental and perfectionist.

Ironically, Bishop Cummins would often voice serious doubts about the wisdom of assigning this or that priest to this or that parish. He'd be told that the Board had no one else to recommend for that assignment. So I directly addressed to the Bishop my idea for expanding the pool of priests for assignment. Bishop Cummins gave me a less than friendly look and explained that expanding the priest pool was not our job.

I often came back to my parish after these four to five hour meetings feeling depressed, frustrated and angry. I was slowly learning that the priest shortage was only the tip of the iceberg. Below the surface were the evils of clericalism, denial, and sexism which cemented the male, celibate clerical system in place.

I wept for parishes that needed and deserved a competent priest. More than once I pleaded with the Board: "Would you want this priest as your pastor or parochial vicar?" They would shrug their shoulders and lament, "What can we do?" They were fearful of questioning the system that forbade discussion of married and women priests. I was no longer willing to keep quiet because I saw the question as one of justice: parishioners have the right to a competent, gifted leader regardless of gender or marital status. But my speaking out was costing me more frustration and less peace of mind.

I finished out my four year commitment on the Personnel Board disillusioned and scandalized because I believed Church authorities were blocking the Holy Spirit's guidance and presence. From my perspective, it was not God who was withholding good shepherds for the flock; it was the boys club of bishops and priests who were stubbornly refusing to change a broken and harmful system. I felt like I was losing my innocence by possessing guilty knowledge of how assignments were made. I did not know what to do about it except to keep speaking out. I kept hoping that Church leadership was not as closed to change as I feared but sadly my fears were confirmed soon after I'd completed my four year term on the Personnel Board.

Chapter Sixteen

DIALOG EFFORT THWARTED

ON MAY 19, 1998, ALL THE PRIESTS of the Oakland Diocese gathered at Transfiguration Parish hall in Castro Valley for an annual day of renewal called Presbyteral Day (presbyter is a fancy word for priest). The committee in charge of planning the day had invited agenda suggestions from the priests, so I sent them one. I suggested that we priests together with the Bishop spend the day reflecting on the priest shortage and what could be done about it. To my delight, the planning committee adopted my proposal. The planning committee sent out the agenda prior to the May 19th meeting to all the priests of the Diocese. The agenda included data on losses and gains in numbers of priests in the Oakland Diocese during the past year as well as projected numbers for the future. The numbers clearly indicated a precipitous drop in the number of priests due to shrinking numbers of newly ordained, retirement, death, and resignations. We priests were asked to prepare for the meeting by answering these two questions: "What response do I have to this information"? And, "What should the Diocese do about it"? I was excited by the prospect of an honest discussion of a crisis affecting not only the Oakland Diocese but most of the Catholic Church in the United States and many other parts of the world. This agenda felt like real progress to me; I could barely contain my gratitude at the planning committee's courage and openness to my agenda proposal.

I arrived for the Presbyteral Day energized and hopeful in spite of my recent depressing experience on the Priest Personnel Board of the Diocese. The facilitator for the day was a psychologist whom I'd never met. I assumed a non-priest outsider was chosen in order to insure impartiality and for his communication and process skills. He divided up the 100 plus priests present into small groups of six to eight members. We were all then handed a sheet with the reflection questions for discussion. I did a double-take after reading the two questions because they were not the same ones sent to us before the meeting. I was shocked to see that the questions had been changed to the following: "What action or behavior can I take now that will prepare me for the next ten years"? And, "What support do I need or can I expect from the Diocese that will help me carry out this behavior"? I thought there must have been some mistake so I stood up to point out that the questions we had in hand were not the same we'd been sent in advance. I added that the changed questions precluded any discussion on the emotional toll the crisis was having on us, and also precluded any discussion of our ideas for how to deal with the priest shortage. The facilitator responded that it was decided that the original questions might have elicited too much strong emotion and controversy so the present questions were substituted to insure a calmer meeting. By now I was so furious that I was shaking. I responded that we all know that a rational discussion of the issue could not happen until there was first an airing of feelings. I said, "we are all adults here and this issue is negatively impacting all of us in one way or another and so we need to have an honest and open discussion including the airing of feelings". No response, case closed!

I sat down feeling so angry I was tempted to storm out of the meeting and head for home. But I stayed put and sat through the meeting incredulous at the manipulation of the agenda to control the discussion, and the fact that only one other priest stood up to support my complaint. I felt totally alone, angry, betrayed, and disillusioned. As I drove home that day, I knew that my relationship with the Diocese's leadership would never be the same. I remember thinking to myself, "my brother priests are numb". I knew from private conversations that deep down, that many of them agreed with me.

Many people within and outside the Catholic Church ask why priests are not more vocal about the need for structural and doctrinal change. Why didn't more of my fellow priests speak up at the Presbyteral Day especially around a topic that directly affected their morale? I will touch on this question in chapter thirty, Dissent, but it bears elaboration here. The number one reason for priests' silence is the belief that it is not a priest's place to question higher authority in the rigidly hierarchical clerical system. Underlying that belief is a fear of rocking the boat and getting punished. Punishments range from the Bishop's disapproval to less chance of promotion be it in rank or pastoral placement. The ultimate punishment could be loss of pay and benefits. As Dostoyevsky articulated in the parable of the Grand Inquisitor in his novel THE BROTHERS KARAMAZOV, human beings in general are all too ready to sacrifice the truth in exchange for security. A priest's desire for security and approval is undergird by the Catholic culture of blind obedience. All Catholics, including priests, are inculcated from childhood with a fawning, uncritical admiration of the clergy especially bishops. Notice how the mood in a room changes when a bishop enters. All too true is the saying that there are two things a bishop never gets: a bad meal and the truth.

Later I learned that it was Bishop Cummins who had asked that the questions for discussion at Presbyteral Day be changed. That didn't surprise me because I knew of his aversion to conflict and controversy, and that he surrounded himself with priests who lacked the courage to be honest with him. The elephant in the room that was being avoided was Pope John Paul II's prohibition of any discussion of alternatives to the all- male, celibate clergy system. The willingness of the vast majority of the world's priests and bishops to obey the Pope on this silencing was a perfect example of a trait of clericalism wherein keeping the Pope father-figure happy was more important to most clergy than making sure every parish and diocese had a sufficient number of competent pastors. I had watched for years the quality and quantity of competent priests diminish, and now I'd experienced firsthand the reason the problem could not even be discussed. I was not only disillusioned; I was angry, and incredulous that this could even be happening.

As I write this in 2014, a few priests and a few bishops are beginning to question the system and the silencing by speaking out for a married priesthood and the ordination of women, but only a few. Meanwhile, parishes are being closed throughout the United States for lack of priests ("nearly 1,400" according to Michael D'Antonio in his book, MORTAL SINS, p. 4). Dioceses are relying heavily on foreign priests to meet their desperate staffing needs. Frequently the foreign priests cannot be understood due to heavily accented English or lack of English. Some foreign priests lack cultural as well as linguistic competence. Some dioceses are lax in their screening processes and fail to sufficiently determine why a particular priest has left his country of origin. For many U.S. bishops, having an ordained priest in a parish is the bottom line regardless of competence. And so more and more Catholics drift away from their Church and morale lowers for those who stay. The bishops shift blame by attributing the causes of these problems to secularism and materialism rather than taking responsibility for their incompetence and rigid adherence to tradition.

The events of that meeting caused me to lose respect for my bishop and fellow priests. I continued to speak up for transparency, dialog, and justice with regard to the priest shortage but over the next six years, other issues began to grab more of my attention, first and foremost, the clergy sex abuse crisis.

Chapter Seventeen

THE STRAW THAT BROKE
THIS CAMEL'S BACK

By 2004, I was in my twelfth year as Pastor of Corpus Christi Parish, Fremont. I knew it would be my last because two six-year terms were the limit according to diocesan policy. These term limits were not strictly enforced but I knew they would be in my case because the Diocese had twice tried to move me to a larger parish. I was feeling a little weary of the demands on a one-priest parish and looking forward to a sabbatical. Priests typically are entitled to sabbaticals after so many years of service and I had been doing parish ministry uninterruptedly for twenty-five years. I had accrued a year's worth of sabbatical time.

By 2004, I was also well aware of the clergy sexual abuse crisis. The crisis had become known nationally and internationally by way of the Boston Globe's getting access to court documents involving the Archdiocese of Boston and then publishing a series of articles naming scores of priest abusers and detailing a large scale cover-up by Cardinal Law and his associates. In the Oakland Diocese, Bishop Vigneron published a report in the Catholic Voice newspaper in which he reported 24 diocesan priests with valid claims against them who sexually abused a known 72 children and teens in 22 parishes between 1950 and 2003. The Bishop also made mention of 11 religious order priests who had been credibly accused. One had the impression from the Bishop's report that this crisis was now behind us due to reforms implemented under the Dallas Charter, the 2002 response of the U.S. Bishops to the abuse crisis. I learned later that Bishop Vigneron underreported the numbers, a chronic problem in bishops' reporting.

By 2004, I was also aware that Msgr. George Francis, with whom I'd lived and worked at St. Bede's in the early 1980's, was a serial child rapist and that several other priests in the Diocese, among them Steve Kiesle, Gary Tollner, Don Broderson, Vince Breen, Bob Ponciroli, Bob Freitas, and Ron Lagasse had sexually abused minors.

None of the above information prepared me for a phone call I received from the Chancellor of the Diocese, Sister Barbara Flannery, early in 2004. Barbara told me there were credible accusations of sexual abuse by two brothers against Fr. Jim Clark (Pastor of Corpus Christi Parish, Fremont, 1964-1984). Barbara said that one of the brothers, Dan McNevin, had told his story to the local newspaper in Fremont, The Argus, and that I should be prepared for its publication in the near future. Sure enough, the story ran on the front page of the local section of the Fremont Argus on March 21, 2004, under the headline, "Ex-altar boy claiming abuse goes public" with a photo of abuse survivor Dan McNevin in front of our parish hall under its big sign, "FATHER JAMES CLARK PARISH CENTER". Talk about the abuse crisis hitting close to home! The McNevin brothers were abused in what was now my home, the parish rectory, and there was at least one other known survivor who was abused by Clark.

I learned from a newspaper story in the Fremont Argus (Dec. 12, 2003) that Dan McNevin had initiated a lawsuit against the Oakland Diocese and bishop John Cummins. Before the March 21st article was published, the journalist contacted me and asked how the parishioners were dealing with these sordid revelations about their former pastor. At the end of our interview, I told the reporter that I would like to meet Dan McNevin. She passed my invitation on to Dan and much to my surprise, he showed up at the front door of the rectory a few days later on March 19th asking to see me. I invited Dan into the dining room where for the next three hours he told me the horrendous story of the abuse that he and his brother suffered at the hands of Fr. Jim Clark thirty years earlier in the very house in which we were sitting.

I was predisposed to believe Dan's story of abuse by the fact that Barbara Flannery at the Diocese found him credible but also by what had been reported in the newspaper story. Also, few people make up stories of abuse. But more persuasive than any of those factors was Dan himself. He spoke to me with eloquence, conviction, and an emotional power that conveyed deep pain, sorrow, and anger. Dan had already had years of therapy which enabled him to keep his sanity, but at times during our meeting I found the power of his emotions frightening. He would cry and at times he would pound the table in anger, but he was always under control.

As horrible as Dan's abuse was, the abuse suffered by his older brother John lasted much longer and with more devastating consequences. John's sexual abuse lasted from adolescence into young adulthood. At some point, the abuse stopped but John continued to suffer severe mental deterioration. He had always been a pious young man and returned once to visit Fr. Clark. Clark quoted to John the Bible passage in which Jesus says: "if your hand leads you into sin, cut it off." John went home and did just that. Luckily, someone found him in time and doctors were able to surgically reattach the hand. It was while visiting John in the hospital that Dan realized for the first time that John had also been abused by Clark. The realization dawned when Clark came into the hospital room to visit John, who when he saw Clark, became agitated and upset.

At the end of his narrative, Dan asked me a big favor. He respectfully acknowledged that this was my home and would understand if I couldn't grant the favor he was about to request. He asked if I would mind allowing him to visit my living room and bedroom upstairs where he and his brother had been sexually molested. I knew right away a visit upstairs for Dan would mean more healing for his wounded psyche since he was now a mature adult returning to the scene of the crimes. Jim Clark had no more power over him. Going upstairs served as a kind of exorcism or purification for Dan, a reminder that he'd travelled a long distance from those days when at age 12 his parish priest was exerting destructive power over Dan and his brother. While upstairs in my private quarters, Dan recalled how the rooms looked thirty years earlier with details about the placement of the furniture. As our visit came to an end, I told Dan I would like to meet his brother if John was open to a meeting, and Dan subsequently arranged for that. Dan thanked me profusely for listening to him and believing in him, and to committing to removing the sign with Fr. Clark's name from the parish center.

After Dan departed, I felt overwhelmed with emotion. I knew it would take some time to sort out my feelings, and I also had a powerful conviction that I would never be the same; that I was forever changed, though it took me several months to tease out the implications of this earthshaking experience. I felt deep compassion for Dan and his brother. All of the stories I'd read and heard about clergy sexual abuse up to that time paled in comparison to Dan's revelation. For the first time, I really "got it" about the devastation sexual abuse causes. I "got it" emotionally to the point that I couldn't look at sexual abuse, priesthood, the Church, my living space, and the way I was living the priesthood in the same way. Though I didn't know it for certain yet, Dan's story was the straw that broke the camel's back and that would lead me within one year into voluntary exile from the priesthood.

One contention of Dan's with which I disagreed on the day of his visit was that the Diocese of Oakland must have known that Fr. Clark had serious problems before he was assigned to Corpus Christi as pastor in 1964. Since Sister Barbara Flannery had said there was no record of previous crimes or misdeeds by Clark, I believed her. Later I learned that Jim Clark had been arrested in a Santa Cruz hotel room, before his assignment to Corpus Christi, for having sex with a 19 year old male (Oakland Tribune, 2/24/2005). Same sex sexual activity was illegal at the time. The fact that Clark was already a priest at the time of his arrest on a morals charge indicates at best a lack of sexual responsibility and a struggle with celibacy. My trust in the candor of Sister Barbara and Bishop Cummins took a big hit. Since then, court documents have revealed this lack of candor over and over again. Church officials lie often to protect the Church's assets and reputation. I felt betrayed and disillusioned again and was more than ever grateful to be starting a sabbatical in August, 2004. However, I want to make it clear that my feelings of betrayal paled in comparison to those of Dan McNevin and all survivors of clergy sexual abuse.

After Clark left Corpus Christi in 1984, he was transferred to St. Anne Parish in Walnut Creek. He died on July 27, 1989, of throat cancer in "good standing" with the Church.

Part III

DECIDING FOR THOSE ON THE MARGINS; 1994 TO THE PRESENT

Chapter Eighteen

SABBATICAL

AFTER TWO SIX-YEAR TERMS as pastor of Corpus Christi Parish, Fremont, and twenty five years as a priest, I was entitled to a year-long sabbatical. Following my meeting with Dan McNevin that spring and after the earlier earthshaking experience at the priest meeting back in 1998 (see chapter sixteen), I knew that a sabbatical not only offered a welcome rest from parish work but also a chance to ask myself some hard questions about my future in the priesthood. Usually when priests are questioning their vocation, they request a "leave of absence". Since I wasn't ready to go public with how disillusioned I felt, I decided to tell people I was taking a six month sabbatical and thus avoid all the concern that would be raised if I said I was taking a leave of absence. Deep down, I assumed I would probably accept another parish assignment after my sabbatical and I wanted everyone else to assume the same.

Having finally nailed down the timing and location for a sabbatical, I spent June and July, 2004, preparing for my leave-taking from the parish. Just the thought of saying goodbye to so many people with whom I'd forged deep bonds of friendship was sad enough but then my life took an apocalyptic turn. In the course of one week that July, my cousin Matt died from liver failure after a long bout with alcoholism, and my dear brother Mark collapsed at work from a seizure and was soon diagnosed with an inoperable malignant brain tumor. Any illusions I had of being in control of my life were suddenly eviscerated. The pain of sad goodbyes was overshadowed by the death of my cousin and the terminal illness of my brother. I departed the parish on July 31ˢᵗ looking forward to a month of vacation prior to heading to Boston on sabbatical.

Beginning in September, I was living in Cambridge, Massachusetts, at the sabbatical students' residence at the Weston School of theology, a graduate school of theology run by the Jesuits. I took two courses at Weston, one on the Gospel of Matthew, the other on discernment of spirits according to St. Ignatius of Loyola. I took a third course across town at Boston College on St. John of the Cross. I enjoyed all three courses but my primary concern was to find a competent spiritual director and start doing some soul searching about my future as a priest. I asked around for recommendations and was led to a Jesuit priest who agreed to meet with me. We agreed to meet every two weeks for three months. Fr. Ken lived up to his good reputation as a spiritual director: a good listener, a person of prayer, common sense and theological/spiritual competence. Ken guided me gently and patiently to getting to the truth within.

In addition to the spiritual direction sessions with Ken, I kept a journal, I prayed, I waited for guidance, I searched, I prayed, I waited. And then I prayed some more. I knew that this process would lead me to one of the biggest decisions of my life. I didn't actually sweat blood as Jesus was said to have done in the garden of Gethsemane, but I felt like I did. The gift of the sabbatical was that it gave me the courage to ask a very painful question: could I continue as a parish priest and maintain my integrity? From that question flowed many others such as: could I continue to represent an institution, the Catholic Church, which systematically enabled and covered up the sexual abuse of children and youth, excluded women from positions of leadership, and demeaned gay and lesbian people by calling them "intrinsically disordered"? Could I continue to raise money for such an institution? Could I continue to encourage religious vocations when I no longer believed that mandated celibacy was a healthy lifestyle for most men and women? If not for time away from parish work, friends, and family, I never would have had the courage and space to ask these scary questions. I think I knew the answer to the questions before I asked them, but by asking them I gradually discovered and received the courage to act on them. Fr. Ken, my spiritual director, often played devil's advocate to help me check on my motivation. When it became clear that I was going to choose to exile myself from priesthood, Ken helped me discern if that choice brought inner peace, the telltale sign of the Holy Spirit's presence.

The peace I experienced once I finally decided not to accept another parish assignment was paradoxically fraught with anxiety about what I would do to make a living and how my decision would be viewed by family and friends. I knew that following my conscience was paramount and that I had to trust that the future direction of my life would be revealed to me over time.

I returned home to California for Christmas, 2004, with the intention of completing the second half of my sabbatical at the Tantur Institute in Israel. In the meantime, some persistent shoulder pain caused by a fall while rock climbing the previous summer grew worse. An MRI revealed a torn labrum in my right shoulder. A surgeon in California strongly recommended I cancel plans for visiting Israel in favor of shoulder surgery. Pain won me over to the surgeon's point of view, much to my chagrin. I underwent surgery in January, 2005, and spent two months convalescing. All the while, I was steeling myself for a visit to the Bishop of Oakland, Allen Vigneron, to tell him of my decision for exile.

On March 15th, 2005, I met with Bishop Vigneron at his office in the chancery. I nervously explained in great detail my decision for exile. I told him of my efforts over several years to initiate discussion and action on issues like the priest shortage and of how my perspective had been radically changed by my visit with Dan McNevin. I added that unless he, the Bishop, was willingly to publicly dialogue on various issues, I could not in good conscience continue to publicly represent the Church as a priest. The Bishop responded that he didn't see any need for public dialogue because the crisis was being addressed by the Pope and bishops. He said he was saddened by my decision but wished me well. He then asked to lead us in prayer. We then parted ways. The only time I heard from him after that was by letter asking me to clarify in writing my status since "exile" didn't fit neatly into any categories of church canon law. My voluntary exile had begun.

The inestimable gift of sabbatical had not ended as I expected but my decision for exile felt true to my convictions and conscience. I felt that I was embarking on a journey whose destination was unknown, a true journey of faith. It was faith that had led me into priesthood and faith that had led me into exile from priesthood. People often asked if I have left the priesthood. I have not left the priesthood but I have chosen to be in exile.

Why "exile"?

Chapter Nineteen

FROM JEWISH EXILE TO CATHOLIC EXILE

During the 6th century BCE, the Israelites spent 70 years in exile in Babylon. While in exile, the Israelites were cut off from the major religious sources of God's presence: no temple, no sacred homeland, no priest, no freedom to worship according to their customs. Exile expressed their experience of being cut off, subjugated, seemingly abandoned by God, grieving for their homeland, in short, mourning and misery. The exile experience of Israel is referred to in many books of the Hebrew Scriptures (the Old Testament) and had an enormous influence on the faith and piety of the Israelites. The Babylonian exile was a time of tribulation and testing often compared to the earlier exodus experience in the desert of Sinai. Exile was much more about faith than about place. It was a human and religious experience which forced the Israelites to understand anew what it meant to be a chosen people.

While on sabbatical, I had read a book entitled THE PRO- PHETIC IMAGINATION by Walter Brueggemann. The author, an Old Testament scholar, helped me name what is happening in the Catholic Church. The Pope and bishops are holding on to their power and misused authority for dear life as they reign over an old order that is "sterile and dying". The first appropriate response to this dying order is to grieve the loss of vitality and integrity in the Church; to weep and mourn in solidarity with those who are being hurt the most by leaders who are deaf to the sounds of suffering: abuse survivors, women, gay people, the divorced, and the disillusioned. To feel and express grief over the sterile status quo places one in exile and subjects one to persecution by the "royals" who are threatened by constructive criticism of their management style and decisions. Brueggemann's term "royals" is used of those in authority, and translates easily to Church leaders in the monarchical structure of the Catholic Church. All my years of growing disillusionment with Church leaders and structure ending in my decision to refuse a post-sabbatical parish assignment finally had a name. Walter Brueggemann's book helped me name my experience and that name is "exile". I was freely choosing exile over conformity with the static status quo of the Roman Catholic priesthood. But Brueggemann reminded me that even exile cannot obliterate the presence of God's glorious presence.

The second appropriate response to the crisis in the Church is doxology, i.e., praise of the living God who hears the cry of the poor and whose compassion and justice are active and everlasting. Brueggemann shows how biblical prophets like Jeremiah energized themselves and others by praise in the midst of misery and seeming hopelessness. Even in the darkness, something wonderful is happening, and this often hidden reality gives reason for hope and encouragement. Brueggemann writes that "doxology is the ultimate challenge to managed power" because it makes clear who God is and what God's priorities are over against the pharaohs of each generation.

Brueggemann's vision, drawn from Scripture and tradition, named for me God's direction for my life: voluntary exile from active priesthood in solidarity with abuse survivors, women and gay people. Brueggemann convinced me that only grief could overcome the pervasive apathy in the Catholic Church. Dan

McNevin had moved me to grief by telling me the story of his sexual abuse as a teenager at the hands of his priest pastor. I had tried in countless ways to awaken my fellow priests and my bishop to act on behalf of those suffering in the Church, but in retrospect, I realized that what was missing for most of them was an emotional engagement with the issues. Even the priests, bishops and lay leaders who understood intellectually that the church is in crisis and that people are suffering did not get it in their guts, in a visceral way that leads to grief, anger, and courage to speak out and work for real reform. So often I'd watched as priests, bishops and lay people shied away from prophetic action because they were afraid. Fear rules the day keeping good people from acting for change even as children, women and gay and lesbian people suffer abuse, degradation and exclusion.

I recall a couple of meetings I had attended before I left on sabbatical. The meetings were organized by a progressive priest of our diocese who invited us to read the book, THE CHANGING FACE OF THE PRIESTHOOD by Donald Cozzens and then gather to discuss the book. About 20 priests showed up for the first two meetings and I remember there being a lot of hope and energy for change in the room. But as the second meeting was wrapping up, our priest moderator asked if we would like to meet a third time to continue the discussion. I said that I would prefer us DO something, to take action instead of talking the problems to death. I suggested, for example, we pick a Sunday in the near future and together refuse to open our parish church doors until our bishop was willing to dialog about the crisis in the church. There was some mild laughter in the room and then the subject was changed. The priests present agreed on a third meeting while I opted out. That was over ten years ago and no action towards reform was ever taken by those priests.

While I'd been on sabbatical, I read a book by Jason Berry and Gerald Renner called VOWS OF SILENCE: THE ABUSE

OF POWER IN THE PAPACY OF JOHN PAUL II. The book exposes the scandal surrounding a Mexican priest named Marcial Maciel Degollado, founder of The Legion of Christ, which involved prolific sexual abuse of seminarians by Marcial abetted by a coverup at the highest levels of the Vatican including Pope John Paul II and Cardinal Ratzinger, now Pope Benedict XVI emeritus. The revelations in that book, credible beyond a doubt, convinced me that only structural reform could resolve the crisis in the Church; that the problems weren't due to a few bad apples but rather to a bad barrel. That book also propelled me in the direction of choosing exile. I felt like the Robert Redford character in the movie "Days of the Condor" when he discovers that his enemies are the men running the CIA for whom he works. The only difference was that my physical life was not in danger. My moral and spiritual life was in great danger from an institution that has completely lost its moral compass by condoning the rape of children and its refusal to hold accountable bishops who sanctioned these atrocities. Although the sexual abuse crisis was the prime motivator in my choice for exile, the mistreatment of women and gay and lesbian persons were also injustices which motivated my decision.

Chapter Twenty

LIFE IN EXILE

AT THIS WRITING, I have been in voluntary exile from active priesthood for ten years. Early on I kept asking myself how I might use my experience and knowledge to advance the cause of structural reform in the Catholic Church. Well meaning friends and family members hoped I would return to active priesthood because "good priests" are so needed. I felt confident about my decision for exile but unsure about how to continue advocating for change. What to do, what to do?

As I wrestled with that question in this uncharted territory of exile, I attended Mass every Sunday at my father's parish, Corpus Christi, Piedmont, located about three miles from my parents' home. After my father died in April, 2008, I continued attending there for two more years. For the most part I enjoyed the parish and found spiritual nourishment there. The people were friendly, generous, and active in ministry within and beyond the life of the parish. The clergy there consisted of the pastor plus two priests in residence. All of them were better than average presiders at Mass and all of them prepared and delivered better than average homilies. What amazed me though was that during the five years I attended Mass there, I never heard a word about the sexual abuse crisis even when it involved the Oakland Diocese. I also heard very few references to the status of women and gay and lesbian people in the Church. The most prophetic homily I heard was given by a visiting priest on the topic of forgiveness. That priest was not invited back because some parishioners let the pastor know they were upset to references to Osama bin Laden in the context of forgiveness. Something was wrong with this picture. The prophetic dimension of the Word of God was missing, a way of preaching and action that challenges the status quo, in this case with regard to the behavior of the institutional Church.

A handful of people in the parish knew that I was a priest but didn't ask me why I didn't have an assignment. The three priests, each of whom I know personally, were well aware of my exile status. I was treated with cordiality but never asked about my stance. They had also read two guest commentaries I'd had published in the Oakland Tribune and several other East Bay newspapers in 2010 and 2011. Those two articles were the fruit of an inspiration I received from Martin Luther King, Jr., but I need to back up a little to provide the context in which that inspiration occurred.

In 2007 I began to volunteer at the Tri-Valley YMCA in Dublin located about 25 miles southeast of Oakland. A friend of mine was the Executive Director there and often called on friends to help out at various Y sponsored events. Eventually I was hired part-time and finally full-time. One event sponsored by the Y is the Dr. Martin Luther King, Jr. Fellowship Breakfast held each year close to the Dr. King's holiday in January.

Since my friend the Executive Director knew that I was familiar with King's writings, she asked me to find a suitable quote for the Fellowship Breakfast. This assignment led me to reread King's famous Letter from Birmingham Jail written in 1963 and addressed "to my dear fellow clergymen." King challenged the passivity of many clergy persons and said that if one believes people are being treated unjustly, one has a responsibility not just to talk about it but to do something about it, an action of public solidarity and advocacy for people suffering injustice. I had to ask myself what I was doing for sex abuse survivors, women and gay people whom I believed were and are being treated unjustly by the Catholic Church. The result of that question to myself was the inspiration to start a weekly protest at the Cathedral of Christ the Light, the Roman Catholic Cathedral of the Diocese of Oakland. My two guest commentaries published by several East Bay newspapers were meant to give publicity to the protest and explain the reason for it. I sent copies of the 2010 commentary to friends, family, many fellow priests and the few bishops I know personally. I received supportive notes and letters from several people including a few priests and even one of the priests at Corpus Christi, Piedmont.

In addition to the weekly protest outside the Oakland Cathedral, I advocate on behalf of abuse survivors, gay people, and women. For example, since I chose exile in 2005, I have met in person with several abuse survivors to offer support and healing. The abuse survivor who was being molested as a little girl while I was an associate pastor at St. Bede Parish in Hayward is now married with children and lives some distance from the Bay Area. I had arranged to meet with her after I went into exile. She told me the horrifying story of her abuse experience and how she had been led to sue the Diocese. The Diocese ended up settling with her out of court because a trial would have revealed more despicable behavior by Diocesan officials and probably led to an even larger payout than the three million dollars she received. More recently, this woman suffered the loss of a baby who was stillborn, and asked me if I would conduct a short funeral service at a cemetery in her town. She asked if I would please not refer to God at all. That request speaks volumes about how profoundly clergy sexual abuse wounds the victim's soul and the capacity for faith in God. I was deeply touched by her willingness to trust me enough to lead the service and I in turn respected her request to keep the word "God" out of it.

I keep informed about the ongoing sexual abuse calamity by daily reading Abuse Tracker, a feature link found at BishopAccoutability.org, that prints news stories, essays, blogs, documents and speeches on clergy sexual abuse from all over the world. For anyone who would like to think the crisis is behind us, I encourage them to click on to this valuable resource.

When I decided with some trepidation to begin the weekly protest on the sidewalk in front of the Cathedral, one of my first quandaries was whether or not to continue to attend Mass at Corpus Christi, Piedmont, or anywhere at all. Sunday Mass has always been a pillar of my faith life because it is there that I experience the Lord Jesus in Word, Sacrament and through the people present. The thought of giving that up was almost unthinkable, at first. But then something happened to change my mind.

One Sunday morning in 2010 just after Mass had ended at Corpus Christi, Piedmont, I was talking to a woman about my ministry in exile and the issues that had led me there. The pastor approached us and overheard the issues I was naming to her. He said to us: "you will never hear me talking about those issues at this church." I asked why and he reiterated, "not here". I was stunned at how direct and explicit he was being but not surprised he felt that way. After all, I'd been attending there for five years and never heard a word about the crisis in the Church.

Later, as I reflected on that interchange with the pastor of my parish, I realized that his position was fairly typical; most Catholics do not hear from their clergy about the sexual abuse crisis. Priests are embarrassed and afraid of the issue so they keep quiet and hope it will pass them and their parish by. This approach is incomprehensible to me. When I was a pastor myself, I spoke out regularly on all aspects of the crisis embroiling the Church. I did so to educate and provide pastoral guidance for people who were reading and hearing about clergy sexual abuse on the news as well about lawsuits, grand juries, and bishops' and popes' statements and cover-ups. Of course in my last parish of Corpus Christi, Fremont, I could hardly avoid addressing the crisis when a former pastor, Jim Clark, was revealed in the local paper as a serial abuser, one of whose victims was speaking out courageously. But I needed to talk about the crisis in church in order to preach the Gospel with integrity and completeness. The Holy Spirit is known as the spirit of truth. For me to avoid controversial topics in my preaching would have been a kind of deception and cowardice. So I was appalled and scandalized by the explicit refusal of the pastor to ever publicly talk about the crisis at his parish, a highly educated and affluent parish in Piedmont. Though I had stopped giving money in the Sunday collection some time earlier, I decided that I could no longer attend a parish that kept silence about sexual abuse by clergy and cover-ups by bishops including the bishops of Oakland. I had also been thinking for some time about the fact that many if not most clergy abuse survivors have had their capacity for faith destroyed by the abuse and cover-up of abuse. The act of going into a Catholic Church for many abuse survivors feels too unsafe and threatening. Since I feel called to solidarity with clergy sex abuse survivors, I decided to begin a kind of eucharistic fast and deprive myself of a huge source of spiritual nourishment since the time of my First Communion at age 7: the Sunday Eucharist/Mass. I miss it terribly!

My first Sunday protest occurred on Sunday, April 11, 2010, at the foot of the front steps of Christ the Light Cathedral on the sidewalk of Harrison St. just down from Grand Avenue across the street from Lake Merritt in downtown Oakland. Dan McNevin, abuse survivor of Fr. Clark, and I had by this time become friends and he arranged for several other abuse survivors to show up that morning in addition to some people from TV stations and newspapers. It was a rainy and windy morning highlighted by a news conference. Dan and I spoke to reporters as did an abuse survivor named Melinda about the crisis, about the cover-up, about the ongoing dangers to children, about the suffering and damage caused by Catholic priests and bishops, and about the need for structural reform. I had prepared a sign and wisely laminated it against the elements that read: STRUCTURAL RE-FORM NOW! INCLUDE THE EXLUDED: WOMEN, GAY PERSONS, ABUSE SURVIVORS. The wind and rain that morning detached the carrying stick from the sign but the sign survived intact and I still carry it each Sunday five years later.

I was nervous that first day. Actually, I was scared to death. My public stance against the Catholic Church brought up feelings of insecurity and vulnerability. To add to the fear factor, a pastor friend of mine had written warning me that there were guards at the Cathedral so I should be careful. Not helpful to hear at all! I wasn't sure what he meant by that but it made me anxious, though not enough to change my plans. There are indeed guards to provide security but they are friendly and leave me and others that join me alone as long as we stay off of church property. That first Sunday in the pouring rain, we tried to start the press conference under the shelter of an overhang in front of some doors but the guard asked us to remove ourselves; not very hospitable of the guard but understandable under the circumstances. I was grateful when that first two-hour protest was over, and not just because it meant getting out of the wind, chill and rain. I knew that I was making a public show of solidarity as called for by Martin Luther King, Jr., and that I was risking criticism and possible censure and other punishment from the Diocese of Oakland.

Sunday after Sunday I show up with my signs (I've added a couple more). Sometimes I'm alone there and sometimes I have company. My other two signs read ENOUGH! and WHAT IF YOU WERE SEXUALLY ABUSED BY A CATHOLIC PRIEST AND NO ONE LISTENED? In the first few months, I always had five or more protesters with me, but as time passed, the numbers dwindled. For the first anniversary in April, 2011, 67 showed up and one TV station sent a reporter and camera. Many Sundays I have been by myself which makes the two hours drag. I much prefer company. Some of those who come out to join me do so moved by the abuse issue, others by the gay marriage issue, and others by the women's ordination issue. We don't usually see too many people from the Cathedral because most Mass attendees enter and exit the church from an underground garage. Plus, the Masses at the Cathedral are not heavily attended. But lots of people drive by and see our signs. Many honk in support, a few in opposition. Passers-by stop to chat and ask what we are about. I have met all manner of people there including homeless folks, tourists, visitors to the cathedral, and lots of locals whom I now recognize easily.

I have many memorable encounters on that sidewalk. Recently a woman saw us and our signs and asked what we are about. After we told her why we are there, she said our protest had her support because years before she and her husband had been big fans of their priest at their parish in Concord. They liked his leadership style and enjoyed his preaching. He had been to their home for dinner. After he'd been removed from the parish, they learned that he had been, as she put it, "an equal opportunity molester". He'd sexually abused several kids in their parish and then was moved on to other assignments. She still stops by churches to pray but can't bring herself to attend Mass anymore. She calls herself a "recovering Catholic". Her story is not uncommon. Each priest abuser has destroyed or diminished the faith of scores of people like that woman.

The current rector (pastor) is my classmate and formerly a good friend of mine. Ray comes out some Sundays to chat, mostly small talk. He doesn't seem to want to talk about the issues which bring me there so I don't try. I have put on hold most of my close priest friendships, including with Ray, because I believe priests who don't advocate for survivors, women and gay people are aiding and abetting injustice. At the same time, I suffer self-doubt that I'm being too self-righteous and judgmental. Then I remember the people like Dan and John McNevin who have to live every day with the shame and pain of their childhood victimization. I wonder how any priest or parishioner can know of such atrocities and remain silent about the status quo in the institutional Church.

I am very grateful for the inspiration I received from Martin Luther King, Jr. that led to my starting the Sunday sidewalk protest five years ago. As I stand there each Sunday for two hours, I often think of abuse survivors by name or imagine them there with me waiting, hoping, and praying for the day when all those being excluded from full participation in the Church will feel welcome, loved and celebrated. I can't wait for the day when I too feel at home again inside the church celebrating the dying and rising of Jesus in praise and thanksgiving to the living God who loves us all, forgives all, and includes all with hospitality and love beyond all telling. For that day to happen, structural reform will have to occur.

In the meantime, I continue to ask what more I could be doing, or if the weekly protest outside the Cathedral is worth continuing.

Part IV

BEYOND THE HEADLINES:
KEY ISSUES FOR STRUCTURAL REFORM

Chapter Twenty-one

THE PRIEST SHORTAGE

I MENTIONED THAT THE PRIEST SHORTAGE was the first issue which roused me to action for reform of the structure of the Catholic Church. I address the topic now in more detail because it is still a crisis that is largely being denied and avoided.

During the 1980's and 1990's, several priests of the Oakland Diocese resigned from ministry, most for some reason relating to mandatory celibacy. Two priests died from AIDS related causes, others left to marry. In the December, 2001, issue of U.S. Catholic, Fr. James E. Sullivan wrote an opinion piece entitled, "Let's Stop giving the priesthood shortage the silent treatment", in which he reported that "over 100,000 priests have left the active ministry during the last 25 years, some 20,000 from the United States alone". He added that the median age of priests has risen from the 40s to the 50s. Now, over ten years later, the median age has risen to the 60s. Most of the article is devoted to the "conspiracy of silence" surrounding the issue due to the Vatican ban on any discussion of married or women priests, and the bishops' enforcement of that ban. In a chilling analysis of the heart of the problem, Fr. Sullivan wrote:

> *Our bishops know that the law of celibacy is not a divine law. Instead of enhancing the preaching of the Gospel—for which it was originally intended, when made a priestly*

requirement at the Second Lateran Council in 1139—
celibacy has now become a hindrance to the divinely
appointed mission. And so, like all laws that have outlived
their usefulness, the bishops realize that it should be changed.
But, sadly, most of them do not ex- press that conviction
openly. They are afraid.
(Sounding Board, U.S. Catholic, for the Dec. 2001 issue)

My awareness both of the fear factor and the shortage itself was raised by my four-year term on the priest Personnel Board during the mid 1990's. At every monthly meeting, we felt the stress of a shortage of qualified priests to fill vacancies in parishes. We often had to "rob Peter to pay Paul" by filling one vacancy by creating another. My repeated pleas for us to discuss the root of the problem, the limited pool of candidates for priesthood, went unheeded because my fellow Board members knew the bishop would not be comfortable with that topic. Keeping the bishop happy is a high priority for most priests. We were conditioned that way in the clerical culture and breaking out of that pattern is not easy or without risk. Many priests are not conscious of how their behavior changes in the presence of the bishop. Deference and unquestioning loyalty is inbred especially for priests who entered seminary in their teens.

In the April 29, 2000, edition of America Magazine, the national magazine published by the Society of Jesus (the Jesuits) in New York City, there was an article entitled, "Are We Killing Our Priests"? which drew my attention. The author, Fr. Francis Dorff began:

Some of the most dedicated priests I know are killing
themselves. They are working themselves to death, unable to
see any other option. The harder they work, the more work
there is for them to do. . . Such priests face the dilemma of

*trying to meet the needs of a growing church while their own
energies and the corps of active priests steadily dwindle...*

Later in the article Dorff gives his reasons for the priest shortage:

*To my mind, the fact that we absolutized the present
exclusive, male, celibate, clerical form of priesthood and
equated it with the essence of the priesthood is the key
reason why we are killing our priests. It colors everything
we do. It leads us to forbid discussion of possible alternative
forms of priesthood and to maintain a priori that they would
be unthinkable. It makes us assume that the workaholic
situation in which we find ourselves could be overcome if
only our priests and we would work a little harder. It blinds
us to the bona fide priestly vocations that do not fit our
present paradigm. By defining the priesthood in terms of the
status quo, we make the increasingly dismal priestly present
our only imaginable future.*

I remember chatting on retreat with the pastor of a large
predominantly Latino, one-priest parish and asking him how he
found the energy to celebrate so many Masses each weekend.
He replied that by the end of the last Mass each Sunday, he felt
"bone-weary" tired. I know the feeling well. It is not healthy for
the people or the priest for one priest to have to celebrate so
many Masses in one day. The fact that so many priests customarily preside at more than three Masses a Sunday explains why
so many do so as if they are reading the phone directory. Bone
weariness sets in so that the priest is barely present anymore. The
quality of preaching and liturgy suffers.

Since I left active priesthood in 2005, the Oakland Diocese
has imported scores of foreign priests primarily from Asia, in particular from India and the Philippines. This policy of proactive

recruitment of foreign priests has met with mixed results at best. Most Catholics do not question the policy unless they cannot understand the priest assigned to their parish. Francis Dorff again on how the Church's exclusivist policy of priestly vocations leads to other problems:

> *Driven by this vision, we multiply ad hoc responses to the problem of the shortage of priests in order to preserve the present form of the priesthood. Our strategies of combining parishes, building megachurches, denying priestly sabbaticals, extending the retirement age of our priests, calling priests out of retirement and importing priests from third world countries to minister to the American church all have this character. For the most part, they are driven less by the pastoral needs and preferences of our people than they are by the organizational need to maintain the present form of the priesthood at all costs. The practice of ordaining married male deacons and appointing women religious and lay men and women as parish administrators can also be seen, not as bold steps towards alternative forms of priesthood, but as necessary accommodations to shore up the priesthood in its present form. When seen in this light, the crisis we are currently experiencing is not rooted in a lack of priestly vocations. It is rooted in a lethal hardening of our categories.*

I would add to this list the practice of allowing Communion services to take the place of Masses in places where there is no priest available to preside at Mass. A Communion service does not require a priest because pre-consecrated hosts stored in the tabernacle are used for Communion. These services resemble a Mass except for the absence of a Eucharistic Prayer with its words of consecration over the bread and wine. Only a priest is authorized to consecrate the bread and wine. I would not allow

Communion services at my parish when I was away because I wanted the people to experience hunger for the eucharist to motivate them to advocate for change in ordination practices. I believe that Communion services enable the bishops to put off dealing with the grave shortage of priests.

The most common response I received when I tried to discuss the roots of the priest shortage was that it was not within our jurisdiction to propose solutions not approved by the Vatican. So we let the people in the parishes be under served or ill-served, and we let the priests be overworked, so as not to offend the Pope and the bishops. Hard to believe but it's all too true and nothing has changed to brighten this bleak picture.

It is scandalous to me that the Pope and the bishops authorize the closing of parishes and cite the shortage of priests while refusing to even discuss the ordination of women and married men to insure an ample supply of priests. Eastern dioceses such as Boston, New York, Detroit, and Cleveland have closed scores of parishes based on this rationale. Some communities have fought these closures by appealing to Rome, mostly to no avail, or by physically occupying their churches. I admire the courage and commitment of these communities but why aren't more Catholics protesting the Vatican's refusal to even talk about alternative vocation pools? And why are most bishops not openly discussing this crisis? They would rather have leaderless parishes and incompetent pastors than question the dictates they receive from on high at the Vatican. The childish passivity of most priests and laypeople enables the Pope and bishops to get away with an egregious abuse of their authority. One of the greatest responsibilities of the Pope and bishops is to ensure that every parish has a competent pastor. Unfortunately, the Church as a whole will not wake up to this tragedy in progress until there is more suffering and neglect. In the meantime people mistake the status quo for the only option.

I weep with sadness and anger whenever I think of the good priests who were chewed up and spit out by the system of mandatory celibacy leading to the priest shortage. Thousands upon thousands of good priests left the ministry solely because they wanted to marry and have a family. Many of these would return to active ministry today if the Vatican changed the celibacy requirement. Under the current system, the priests suffer, the people in the parishes suffer, and the mission of Jesus suffers.

I will close this chapter with another powerful quote from Francis Dorff :

> *Does God want us to keep heading in this direction?*
> *Personally, I have a hard time believing that God wants*
> *us to keep heading in a direction that is killing our*
> *priests, depriving us of the sacraments and threatening to*
> *undermine our identity as a priestly people. I believe that,*
> *through the shortage of priests, God is calling us to be open*
> *to experiencing a paradigm shift—a radical communal*
> *conversion in how we understand ourselves as a priestly*
> *people and the priests who serve us. I believe that being*
> *faithful to that call will require that we openly entertain*
> *all the options of alternative forms of priesthood and shift*
> *our mode of discernment on the question from a narrow,*
> *authoritarian one to the broad, dialogical process which*
> *animated the Second Vatican Council. I firmly believe that*
> *such courageous faithfulness will let us experience anew the*
> *depths of the priestly ministry that is at work within us and*
> *allow us to express that mystery in creative new forms as a*
> *new millennium dawns.*

Chapter Twenty-two

CLERICALISM

CLERICALISM, THE WIDELY HELD BELIEF that priests and bishops are superior to lay people, has caused a scandal which often goes unreported: the low standards set for parish priests and the resultant widespread unprofessional conduct. Some priests get away with appalling behavior and drive people away from the Church while the bishop looks the other way unless the misbehavior involves stealing parish money.

Two years ago I had lunch with some friends including a priest with whom I'd worked for years. I told them the story of a friend of mine who was sexually assaulted by a priest in her parish when she was a teen. The priest was removed from that parish but reassigned several times to other parishes where he abused many more youth. My priest colleague thought that this abuser priest was worthy of a second chance and that the bishop did right to give him that second chance. I was incredulous. I said, "How could you even consider taking such a huge risk"? He replied that mercy and compassion demanded that such risks be taken. The fact that many children lives were decimated by that risk-taking did not seem to be of ultimate concern to this priest.

Why was my colleague so blind so the moral imperative to protect the children? The answer: clericalism, pure and simple. Priests are taught they are special, treated as if they are special, and many believe it, expect it, and act like it. The mindset of clerical-

ism carries with it a sense of entitlement, privilege and special-
ness. Priests are called by the exalted title of "father", they wear
distinctive clothing, and are accorded unearned trust and respect
by most Catholics. In addition to the exalted status of priests
within the church and the greater community, priests are set
apart by a lifestyle trait unique in our culture: priests are obliged
to make a promise of celibacy which prohibits them from not
only marriage but any sexual activity at all. I will address celibacy
in another chapter but for now I want to highlight it as a key part
of the structure of the Catholic Church that fosters clericalism by
creating a false but exalted image of the ordained clergy as men
immune to the need of a spouse and immune to the need for
sexual intimacy. Clericalism then is a mindset of superiority that
believes clergy (ordained priests and bishops) are special by virtue of their calling. The clericalism mindset is rooted in Church
structure and law.

Currently, the way the Catholic Church is structured is hierarchical with the Pope having absolute authority, accountable
to no one but God. The bishops have in theory some collegial
(shared) authority but they rarely if ever go against the wishes
of the Pope. Not only is the Catholic institution's structure top-
down, it's also extremely secretive and comprised only of men. In
short, the Church's structure is monarchical, medieval, and patri-
archal. It is also clericalized, meaning that there are two classes in
the Catholic Church: the clergy and everyone else. Everyone else
are the laity and within the laity a special group called "religious".
The religious are comprised of nuns/sisters and brothers, all of
whom belong to religious orders. Sisters and brothers take vows
of poverty, chastity, and obedience which set them apart from the
rest of the laity or non-religious. The clergy are the upper class,
the laity the lower class, with the religious somewhere in between. The clergy possess most of the power and influence in the
Church and they are looked upon as closer to God by most of

the lay people. This two-tiered church structure is not mentioned in the Bible. Jesus did not call for a clergy or even a priesthood. Jesus in fact, warned against church authorities receiving special titles such as "father" or the wearing of distinctive dress to symbolize authority.

When it comes to the structure of the Catholic Church, most Catholics accept it as a given and assume that the men in charge are obedient to God and therefore will use their authority wisely, and that this has been the case for two thousand years so why change it now. Most Catholics are indoctrinated at an early age with an attitude of passivity regarding church structure and tradition. Until recently, that is why the Pope and bishops did not receive much pushback from rank and file Catholics. But with the ongoing crisis of the sexual abuse of children and youth by priests and bishops in every country on earth, more and more Catholics are asking why these scandals are so prevalent, universal, and ongoing. Unfortunately, they too blindly rely on the answers provided by the very men running the institution: the Pope and the bishops, aka the foxes guarding the hen house.

When the U.S. bishops gathered in Dallas in 2002 to address the sexual abuse crisis in the American church, they invited some non clergy outside experts to address them, but it was the bishops themselves, with the Pope's approval, who decided how to solve the problem. They were not deterred by the fact that 66% of their members had reassigned abuser priests who went on to abuse more children and youth. Not one of these bishops has ever been held accountable for his crimes except Cardinal Bernard Law of Boston whose "punishment", after a public outcry over an extended period of time, was a good salary and a job as honorary pastor of an ancient Roman basilica. The bishops dismiss such criticism by contesting that at the time they were reassigning abuser priests, they believed, on expert advice from psychologists, that these priests could be rehabilitated. But such a rationale flies in the face of basic common sense and morality. Would any parent take such a risk of reassigning a priest who had abused a child? And is a priest who has molested a child worthy of a second chance? Most of the psychologists consulted did not recommend giving priest abusers access to children or youth. It was the clericalism mindset which framed the bishops' way of understanding and handling this crisis.

The bishops' argument that they didn't know that abuser priests could not be rehabilitated is contradicted by Father Gerald M. C. Fitzgerald, founder of the religious order, Servants of the Paraclete in 1947, who worked with troubled priests. Fitzgerald wrote to dozens of bishops in the 1950's (yes, the 1950's!) that most abuser priests were dangerous and unrepentant and therefore should never be allowed near children. He advised Vatican officials in 1962 and Pope Paul VI a year later that pedophile priests should be removed from the priesthood.

I believe that the primary reason for the reassignment of priests, which continues today, is clericalism, the illusion that priests and bishops are specially blessed by God and therefore superior to others, and therefore should not be judged by the same standards as non-clergy.

The leadership structure of the Church at present is secretive, exclusively male, celibate (in theory), and elitist due to the deeply ingrained sin of clericalism. The people least capable and least inclined to reform such an unhealthy structure are the bishops and priests themselves. Not only do most of them not see the need for reform; they don't want to change a system that affords them unlimited power, authority and privilege. The Pope and bishops keep blaming the Church's problems, including the sexual abuse of children and youth by priests and bishops, on moral weakness, sin, secularism, relativism, materialism, and corrupt cultures. They counsel the need for more prayer, repentance and discipline while children continue to be molested by clergy.

Priests continue to be reassigned, and bishops continue to get away with criminal behavior. I am convinced that the crisis will continue until bishops are held accountable and there is structural change that gets to the core causes of the crisis: secrecy, patriarchy, mandatory celibacy, and clericalism.

My experience on the Personnel Board of the Oakland Diocese in the mid 1990's taught me that the top down structure of the Church produces the commonly held expectation that real reform can only happen from the Vatican. And yet the Vatican leaders are the least able to change a system that they are bound and determined to maintain and protect. Yves Congar, a French Dominican priest whose writings had a major influence on several Vatican II documents, was forbidden to teach for a time in the mid 1950's. In a letter to his mother, he wrote: "... the whole history of Rome is about insisting on its own authority and the destruction of everything that cannot be reduced to submission."

Robert M. Hoatson, an ex-priest, abuse survivor and founding member of National Survivor Advocates Coalition, after living for many years first as a Christian Brother and later as a priest writes that,

> . . . the clerical culture is highly dysfunctional. . . This is
> not a culture that needs tweaking or reform. It must be
> eliminated. The structures, policies, and practices of clericalism
> that have fostered the serial sexual abuse of hundreds of
> thousands of children, teenagers, and vulnerable adults
> and corrupted one of the world's great religions are still in
> place and will be for the indefinite future because the guys
> in charge like the power they have. While the church and
> priesthood implode, the power brokers battle to keep the
> structures in place so they can stay in power. And, the black
> and white code of silence is upheld. Except in Kansas City
> and Philadelphia, where courageous prosecutors said enough

is enough and indicted not just a bishop, priests, and a lay teacher but a corrupt, dysfunctional, arrogant, and sick clerical culture.

(QUOTED FROM THE *VOICE FROM THE DESERT* BLOG ON BISHOPACCOUNTABILITY.ORG, 3/31/2012)

Resistance to structural reform within the Church is so formidable that to even suggest it is to risk censure. My efforts to raise the question of structural reform while I was still an active priest were met with a wall of resistance so high and thick that I began to feel powerless, and frustrated. I remain convinced that structural reform is the answer but that it will not happen from within. It will take a lot more suffering in the form of scandals, lawsuits, bankrupt dioceses, and an awakened and emboldened laity to begin the process of structural change. Almost three billion dollars has been paid out in lawsuits just in the U.S. alone since 2002 and still the bishops and Pope are in denial that more reform is needed. Structural reform is the answer to a question more people need to be asking, i.e., how do we even begin to solve this crisis?

Chapter Twenty-three

CLERGY SEXUAL ABUSE

A RECURRING THEME DURING MY TIME as a priest of the Diocese of Oakland was the gradual revelation of sexual abuse by priests and cover-ups by Bishops Begin and Cummins, the first two bishops of the Diocese from its inception in 1962 until 2003 when Cummins retired. In four of the five parishes where I served as a priest, there have been at least one priest abuser.

I alluded earlier to Msgr. George Francis, the pastor at my second parish assignment, St. Bede's, who turned out to be a serial pedophile over a forty year period. I first learned of George's dark history approximately fifteen years after I had left St. Bede's from a newspaper story of November 15, 2002, in the Fremont Argus, about two female victims of his sexual abuse who held a news conference on the steps of the church announcing a lawsuit against the Diocese of Oakland. Both women had been parishioners at St. Bede's as children. The suit was being brought by Jennifer Chapin who was being abused by George during my time in the parish in the early 1980's. The other woman, Terrie Light, had been abused by George a generation earlier beginning in 1959 when she was 7 in an era when dioceses made secret payments to abuse victims while swearing victims and their families to secrecy. I remembered Jennifer's parents well. Her father had been a lector and I had fond recollections of chatting with him and his wife after Sunday Mass. They had been close friends of

Msgr. Francis and trusted him completely even allowing Jennifer to spend extended hours alone with him. She suffered sexual abuse beginning at age 5 in 1979 and continuing into 1982 when she was 8. George Francis was around 70 years of age in 1979.

The Diocese of Oakland ended up settling with Jennifer in 2005 by paying her $3 million (L.A.Times, Feb., 2005), a state record for a diocese's payment to an individual. I later learned from Jennifer that the Diocese had settled with her to avoid a trial in which a former neighbor of Jennifer's family was ready to testify that she had reported to the Diocese seeing George Francis visiting Jennifer alone at her family's home.

Since I chose voluntary exile from the priesthood in 2005, I have met with Jennifer and Terrie to offer support and encouragement. During my meeting with Jennifer, her first question to me was: how could I have not known of her abuse since I lived in the same rectory with George, her perpetrator. George, like most sexual abusers, was very secretive. He had been abusing girls for forty years and was extremely guarded about his private life. During my four years sharing a rectory with George, his quarters were on the ground floor while mine and the two other priests were upstairs. I never saw or heard anything that would raise a suspicion that George was abusing Jennifer.

Neither Jennifer nor Terrie could begin to face their painful memories of abuse until years after the abuse occurred. Both women are courageous even as their lives continue to suffer the devastating effects of sexual molestation by a priest. Their victimization is all the more regrettable given the fact that Church authorities knew of George's criminal ways before either of them fell prey to his perverse behavior. There are 11 known victims of George Francis, the first dating back to 1938 (Fremont Argus, 11/15/2002).

As the shocking news of Msgr. Francis' secret life sank in, I felt angry that the Diocese had never removed George from the parish or the priesthood. He died in a hospital in 1998 after suffering a stroke several years earlier.

Besides St. Bede's, three other parishes in which I served as a priest also had clergy abusers assigned to them: Fr. Steve Kiesle and Fr. Bob Freitas at Our Lady of the Rosary, Union City, Fr. Don Broderson and Fr. Ron Lagasse at St. Raymond, Dublin, and Fr. James Clark at Corpus Christi, Fremont (see chapter 17). St. John Vianney had a priest who was accused, removed from ministry, and later reinstated due to lack of credibility of the one accusation.

The Oakland Diocese like all other dioceses across the nation and world does not voluntarily divulge its dirty secrets. If it were up to many of the clergy, bishops and priests included, all of this sordid history would still be shielded from the public. Like a majority of bishops, some priests place protecting the reputation of the Church ahead of protecting children from sexual abuse. Many of the details to this day are still a secret and protecting the secrets has cost the Oakland Church untold millions of dollars in legal fees. What is known is due to the courage of survivors, their families and friends, the courts and the news media.

In a March, 2008, two-part series, MediaNews reporters published an in-depth study in several East Bay newspapers on the sordid history of clergy sexual abuse in the Diocese of Oakland. Their findings, culled from court documents, Church files, and many others sources, revealed that 64 accused priests and religious brothers had served in the diocese between 1950 and 2003. Most of the priests who abused children and youth have never been prosecuted because of statutes of limitations and many have still not been publicly named. None of the diocesan officials who moved abuser priests from parish to parish and arranged private settlements to victims, and paid diocesan lawyers to savagely attack victims in court, have ever been prosecuted. Bishop

John Cummins, the bishop who ordained me a priest, retired "honorably" and continues to preside at religious services and parish and diocesan events. Justice has not been served for victims because the full truth has not been revealed. The two bishops and their priest assistants who moved abusive priests from parish to parish to parish have not been held publicly accountable. Church leaders speak as if the problem is behind us and see no need to dredge up the past. The problem is that the past is still present. The hundreds of abuse survivors in the Oakland Diocese cannot just put their trauma behind them. They need and deserve generous support beginning with an acknowledgement of what happened to them, that it was not their fault, and that the Church will do all in its power to offer support, healing, and justice.

Earlier I wrote that many priests and most bishops are in denial about the depth of this crisis. Among those who acknowledge the depth of the crisis, there is often an absence of emotional understanding of how damaging sexual abuse is, especially when perpetrated by a priest. Abuse survivors never get over the trauma they experienced. Experts believe that the majority never go public with their experiences of abuse because of fear, shame, and guilt. I only awoke emotionally to the damage inflicted by clergy sexual abuse of a child when Dan McNevin told me of his abuse experience (see chapter 17).

Most people assume that the Church has for the most part fixed the problem by the reforms instituted by the Dallas Charter in 2002 following the world-wide publicity generated by the Boston Globe expose regarding clergy sexual abuse in Boston and the cover-up that accompanied it for decades. The Church has spent and continues to spend millions to get the public to believe that the abuse crisis is all a thing of the past. Many U.S. bishops pride themselves on how well the Church has done in addressing and solving the crisis. In fact, there is ample evidence that the problem is not fixed at all. All one needs to do to confirm this is to check the up-to-date posts on the website Abuse Tracker. Although there are fewer cases of clergy sexual abuse now due to greater scrutiny and awareness, I have no doubt that the abuse of children by clergy continues because the root causes have not been addressed: secrecy, clericalism, mandatory celibacy, sexism, and an outmoded sexual ethic.

Richard Sipe, a long-time advocate for victims of clergy abuse, reported at a conference at Santa Clara University on May 11, 2012: "Sexual abuse of minors by Roman Catholic clergy is a long-standing problem. It is historical but not 'history'—the crisis is not over as some bishops and others declared in 2004 and since." Sipe reminded the audience that as far back as 1992, he had told the First National Conference for Victims and Survivors of Roman Catholic Clergy Abuse held in Chicago: "The crisis of sexual abuse by Catholic bishops and priests now visible is the tip of the iceberg. When the whole story of sexual abuse by presumed celibate clergy is told, it will lead to the highest corridors of Vatican City."

And so it has, as witnessed by the close ties between Pope John Paul II and Fr. Marcial Maciel Degollado, disgraced and now deceased founder of the Legion of Christ. In 2004 while I was on sabbatical, I read VOWS OF SILENCE, The Abuse of Power in the Papacy of John Paul II, by Jason Berry and Gerald Renner. The authors document how eight former seminarians accused Maciel of sexual abuse. One of them, Juan Vaca, wrote to Pope John Paul II detailing his abuse at the hands of Maciel. Yet as late as 2004 the Pope presided at a ceremony in Rome in honor of Maciel. Maciel was protected by the Pope because of his prodigious fund raising, his ability to recruit seminarians for the priesthood, and his generous donations to high level Vatican officials including the then Secretary of State, Angelo Sodano. Only in 2006, after Pope John Paul II's death, did Pope

Benedict XVI discipline Maciel by ordering him to a life of prayer and penance. Maciel died in 2008. After his death, it was revealed that he had two secret families, fathered several children, and sexually abused two of his own sons. (National Catholic Reporter, Feb. 22, 2008). Not only are the facts of Maciel's abuse well documented in Berry's book; a recent Frontline documentary on PBS television, The Secrets of the Vatican, covers the crimes of Maciel including interviews with Juan Vaca and one of Maciel's sons.

At that same Santa Clara University conference, Fr. Thomas Doyle said: "In spite of the assurances from Church officials that the worst is behind us, this is clearly delusion and not reality." Fr. Doyle coauthored a report to the U.S Bishops back in 1985 warning them that they had a significant problem on their hands but Doyle's report was largely ignored. Doyle's involvement in this issue is extensive and multi-faceted. On May 11, 2012 he said this at Santa Clara:

> *In the United States the Catholic bishops have created*
> *a number of programs and policies and have aggressively*
> *implanted their 'Zero Tolerance' policy. In spite of these*
> *policies and the expensive public relations efforts they have*
> *implemented, the attitude of the bishops as a collective group*
> *has not only not changed but it has gotten worse. Their*
> *disdain for the victims has become more and more obvious.*
> *The true measure of their understanding of the horrific*
> *nature of the issue and their commitment to change is not*
> *the programs, policies, documents or speeches they generate*
> *but their unqualified attitude of compassion toward the*
> *victims and this is scandalously lacking. The bishops simply*
> *don't get it or if they do get it, they don't care.*

Not until the abuse crisis made national headlines in 2002 did the U.S. Bishops begin to address the abuse crisis in a concerted manner. The bishops commissioned a study of the causes of the abuse crisis by the John Jay School of Law in New York City. John Jay cited many causes but primarily blamed the crisis on the culture of the sixties. This finding has become the fodder for jokes and disbelief because it is so ludicrous. There is ample evidence of clergy sexual abuse that happened prior to the 1960's, and since the Boston meltdown, clergy sexual abuse has been exposed around the world in scores of countries: Ireland, the Netherlands, Belgium, Germany, Austria, Australia, Canada, Mexico, and Chile have suffered an epidemic of abuse.

Some Catholic critics argue that the problem is no worse in the Catholic Church than in other churches, religions, and institutions such as schools and the Boy Scouts. However the facts reveal that in every diocese where there has been a grand jury investigation that gained access to diocesan secret files, the rate of abuse is closer to 10% of priest abusers than the John Jay's reported figure of 4%. Informed critics of the John Jay Report point out that the John Jay investigators obtained their statistics from Church officials who are chronically prone to lies, distortions, and minimization. Pope Francis in mid 2014 opined that 2% of clergy have sexually abuse children and youth.

Even if one believes that "only" 4% of priests abuse children and youth, is that not a scathing indictment of the Catholic priesthood which, according to its mystique, is supposed to be rooted in a call to holiness by the standards of Gospel love and justice? Nevertheless, the fact is that one in ten priests abuse children and youth in most dioceses. At present, the Diocese of Oakland has approximately 150 diocesan priests which means that statistically 15 of those men have or will abuse minors. That is a shocking and alarming statistic given the devastation--psychological, emotional, physical, spiritual-- abuse of even one child or teenager wreaks on the life of that boy or girl: a life of panic, major difficulty with trust, sleep problems, mental illness, social adjustment problems, profound loneliness, and often an inability to believe in God or go near a church. Drug and alcohol abuse are common among abuse survivors and many abuse survivors commit suicide overwhelmed by fear, shame, guilt and powerlessness. Now I know this first hand because of relationships I have formed with childhood abuse survivors, some of them now in the 40's and 50's, who still struggle with these issues.

Four to ten per cent of priests sexually abusing minors is shocking in itself but add to that the sixty-six per cent of U.S. bishops who, when presented with a priest under their authority guilty of sexual abuse, chose to move the priest to a new assignment rather than call the police and remove the priest from ministry and from the priesthood. Since 2002 when the U.S. bishops adopted a zero tolerance policy under their Dallas Charter, several more bishops have left abusive priests in ministry and not called the police, e.g. Cardinal George in Chicago, Bishop Finn in Kansas City, Missouri, and Archbishop Nienstedt in Minneapolis-St. Paul, Minnesota.

On June 22, 2012, Msgr. William Lynn, a former aide to the Archbishop of Philadelphia, was found guilty of child endangerment for reassigning priests he knew to be abusers. Lynn's conviction marked the first time a Church official was tried and found guilty for his role in reassigning priests who were known abusers.

In an expose published in Rolling Stone Magazine in September, 2011, Sabrina Rubin Erdely wrote: "In bringing conspiracy charges against Lynn, the Philadelphia district attorney is making a bold statement: that the Catholic hierarchy's failure to protect children from sexual abuse isn't the fault of an inept medieval bureaucracy, but rather the deliberate and criminal work of a cold and calculating organization. In a very real sense, it's not just Lynn who is on trial here. It's the Catholic Church itself." She also wrote: "In sheltering abusive priests, Lynn wasn't some lone wolf with monstrous sexual appetites, as the church has taken to portraying priests who molested children. According to two scathing grand jury reports, protocols for protecting rapists in the clergy have been in place in Philadelphia for half a century, under the regimes of three different Cardinals. Lynn was simply a company man, a faithful bureaucrat who did his job exceedingly well. His actions were encouraged by his superiors, who in turn received orders from their superior--an unbroken chain stretching all the way to Rome."

In Ireland, five different studies have revealed an epidemic of abuse in various parts of that country. Recently, the Prime Minister of Ireland publicly criticized the Vatican for contributing directly to the crisis by its demands for secrecy and refusal to hold erring bishops accountable.

The International Criminal Court at The Hague was recently presented with a case against the Catholic Church for human rights abuses against children throughout the world. Though it refused to hear the case on jurisdictional grounds, abuse survivors will continue their efforts to hold the Vatican accountable. Governments in Belgium and the Netherlands have launched investigations into Church handling of clergy sexual abuse in those countries.

The Bishop of Kansas City, Robert Finn, went on trial in September, 2012, for waiting six months to report a priest, Fr. Sean Ratigan, of his diocese who possessed child pornography. Bishop Finn had received a letter from the school principal at Fr. Ratigan's parish listing concerns from teachers and parents about this priest's behavior around children. Bishop Finn failed to intervene. A jury found him guilty of a misdemeanor for failing to report this priest to the police, a priest whom he knew possessed child pornography. Bishop Finn has not been removed from his position.

When I step back and think about all the various aspects of the ongoing clergy sex abuse crisis, I ask myself how can this be happening in the church to which I have devoted my life? How did we get from Jesus proclaiming the good news of the Kingdom of God to a Church whose leadership systematically sacrifices the lives of children and youth for the sake of trying to protect its reputation? To understand the "how" and the "why", I have done extensive reading about clergy sexual abuse.

Recently I read CHILD SEXUAL ABUSE AND THE CATHOLIC CHURCH by Marie Keenan, a Ph.D. scholar and psychotherapist in Dublin, Ireland. Her book is the most in-depth and exhaustive study of the topic I've seen to date. She convinced nine Irish priests in treatment for abusing children and/or youth to cooperate in her study.

Keenan repeatedly asserts the complexity of child sexual abuse by clergy and writes that "single factor theories are inadequate at explaining fully child sexual abuse". (p. 94)

Her research finds that "Catholic clergy represent a relatively distinct and atypical group of child sexual offenders whose offending must be considered in the situational and contextual circumstances of their lives as ministers of the Roman Catholic Church." (p. 73)

So rather than only understanding clergy offenders from each one's psychological profile, Keenan studies several factors unique to priesthood such as Church teaching on sexuality, mandatory celibacy, seminary training, obedience, loneliness and isolation, ignorance about sexuality, clerical loyalty, secrecy, negative attitudes towards women, and a priests' power relations with lay people and bishops.

Keenan concludes that priests are set up for failure and that "the Church has yet to deal with the institutional and structural issues that the abuse crisis has brought to the surface." (p. 257) She zeroes in on the celibacy question:

Is it not cruel to demand lifelong sexual abstention from human beings, despite all the research hinting at serious problems with such lifelong practices, especially when not voluntarily chosen? Against easily available scientific and social scientific knowledge and advice, the Church still continues to teach its clergy to abstain sexually. Knowing that such demands of sexual abstention are totally unrealistic, this is exactly where one aspect of institutional hypocrisy comes in as an explanation. The Church still promotes an institutional practice that is bound to fail. Cruelty and abuse are bound to arise from such impossible tasks. (p. 263)

Of course not all priests abuse children but many priests struggle greatly in their longing for sexual and emotional intimacy. Several factors contribute to the sexual deviance of priests who abuse minors. Of the nine offending priests Keenan studied, six had been abused themselves. These men entered seminary suffering from "corrosive shame" that in turn led to emotional isolation. Two of the offenders she studied entered seminary to avoid sexuality altogether. All felt isolated in their struggles and felt constrained to talk about them with anyone but their confessor. All tended to intellectualize their feelings of loneliness, isolation, anger, frustration and longing, thus making themselves vulnerable to being controlled and driven by those same feelings.

Keenan's observations resonate with my own. The priest abusers I have known and/or worked with all appeared limited in their relational and intimacy skills. Several used alcohol as a coping mechanism which in turn no doubt lowered their inhibitions when tempted to act out sexually with minors. I'm guessing that some of these men were abuse victims themselves based on the high incidence of victimization by those who abuse minors.

Marie Keenan's exhaustive study of child sexual abuse by Catholic clergy points the way to resolving a very complex problem:

> *Judging from the public outcry by Catholics throughout the Western world, including the clergy themselves, the abuse problem by clergy and the response to abuse by the Church hierarchy and the Vatican, is one that will only be settled by structural reform, a new more critical theology and a new ecclesiology. (p. 266)*

Chapter Twenty-four
MANDATORY CELIBACY

MANY CATHOLICS OF MY GENERATION and older have experienced our sexuality as a mixed blessing. How could we not, given the fact that Catholic teaching on human sexuality devalues the body and too often views sex as a necessary evil permissible only for the procreation of children. When celibacy was mandated for all priests of the Roman rite in the 12th century (there are several smaller groups of Catholics with traditions developed in the eastern part of the Roman Empire whose clergy are allowed to marry), the Church was teaching that priests were better off without sex, wives, and families. What a leap from the time of Jesus, a Jew, who chose twelve Jewish men as his Apostles, all of them likely married. We know Peter was married because of the Gospel story in which Jesus healed Peter's mother-in-law of an illness.

How the Catholic Church learned to devalue the body, sexual desire and activity is too complicated to explain in detail but a few influential factors are worth citing here. Classical Greek philosophy, specifically Platonic ideas, placed a higher value on the spiritual dimension of life than on the material/physical dimension in the human quest for union with the divine and the search for perfection. Platonic thought is extremely dualistic in its exaltation of spirit over matter. St. Augustine gravitated to Platonic philosophy as it spoke to his own painful maturation process. His negative teachings on sexuality had a major influence on Catholic thought. Another contributing factor to Catholic negativity about sex was misogyny, the fear and denigration of women. Influential theologians like St. Thomas Aquinas argued from scripture, philosophy, and bad science that women are inferior to men and a potential threat to men's spirituality because of their sexual allure. These strains of thought gradually infiltrated Catholic thinking to the extent that Church doctrines today still reflect these negative influences, e.g. the ban on women's ordination, the prohibition of sex outside of heterosexual marriage, and mandatory celibacy for priests and bishops of the Roman rite.

During my twenty-five years as a parish priest, the topic of celibacy was addressed at retreats and during spiritual direction. Although celibacy was considered a calling separate from the call to priesthood, in practice they were treated as one and the same. The Church maintained this distinction of two separate callings because there have always been priests of other than the Roman rite who are allowed to marry. The assumption of priest leaders was that celibacy was a challenging but positive calling for the good of the Church. The theory went that by sacrificing sex, marriage and family, the priest was freer to devote himself fully to the service of the people. We were taught that any difficulties could be overcome by God's grace. I did not question this long held discipline/practice because I looked upon priesthood as a sacred calling and held the priesthood in high esteem. My psychosexual consciousness had been developed within the fear and shame based context of Church teachings on sexuality and reinforced by my father's admonitions. The only explicit command I received from my father regarding my sexuality was: "don't play with yourself!" I was naïve, idealistic, and very desirous of doing what was right. If celibacy was good enough for Jesus and St. Paul, and if the Church taught that it was a higher spiritual calling than marriage, then I was willing to promise to live celibately, i.e. to abstain from any and all sexual activity.

At the time I chose to enter the seminary in 1974 at age 25, I had dated several women and had been intermittently sexually active like most young men of my generation. What drew me to priesthood was not celibacy but the person and teaching of Jesus. I trusted that the Church knew best with its requirement of celibacy for priesthood. To my mind, the celibacy of priests represented an ideal of total commitment to God and the Church. I'd always looked up to priests and assumed they kept celibacy because somehow the strength came with the sacrament of Holy Orders. In retrospect, I realize that my willingness to sacrifice sexual intimacy to follow Jesus as a priest was partly motivated by guilt about my sexual experiences and some disillusionment resulting from my intimate relationships with women. Although strongly attracted to women, I felt that celibacy would free me from the downside of sex, dating, and marriage.

In retrospect, I realize that I brought with me into the seminary a fair amount of guilt and shame around my own sexuality. I half expected not to be accepted by the seminary because I had had premarital sex, a mortal sin in the eyes of the Church. Though I'd had a few girlfriends including a relationship that lasted several years, I did not have much confidence in my relationship skills and was definitely out of touch with my own emotions. So the idea of giving up sex, a spouse and family had an upside for me: I'd become closer to God and not ever have to fail at intimacy.

It did not take long to discover that the life of a diocesan priest is a very lonely one. At the end of the day, I would come home to my bedroom to sleep each night alone. I did not choose the priests with whom I lived, and although I got along with all of them to greater and lesser degrees, I was close friends with none of them. There was often camaraderie with the other priests but sometimes alienation too, particularly at St. Bede's.

Not surprisingly, my first conscious awareness of finding celibacy burdensome was during my second assignment (St. Bede's) where the workload was heavy and some of the other priests uncongenial. I felt extremely lonely much of the time and my will power to resist physical and emotional attachments with women began to weaken. I belonged to a priest support group called Jesus Caritas wherein I met with four priest friends monthly for two days. I was open with them about my struggle to stay celibate and they were encouraging and supportive. I prayed daily, took a day off each week, and exercised regularly, but the loneliness of the work and living situation persisted and I periodically became emotionally and physically involved with adult women. I felt horrible about breaking my promise to be celibate and guilty about the secrecy and duplicity of my actions. I finally knew I had to get help so I sought out a therapist who helped me get up the courage to ask for a transfer. I left St. Bede feeling broken and sad but hopeful that my new assignment in Walnut Creek would provide me a fresh start and renewed strength to live celibately. Sadly, I could not yet see that beneath my struggles was a healthy desire for physical and emotional intimacy and a sustained and faithful partnership with a woman.

The Church requires of aspirants to the priesthood two gifts: a call to priesthood and a call to celibacy. But in the training for priesthood, the call to celibacy is not articulated beyond generalizations such as, God supplies the gift and the priest needs only to be open to the gift by prayer, discipline and a balanced lifestyle.

As I mentioned earlier, I first began to struggle to keep celibacy during my second parish assignment, a time of overwork, loneliness, and lack of emotional support from my fellow priests in the rectory. But even if those negative factors had not been present, the human need for emotional and physical intimacy was also a major factor in my struggles to remain celibate.

Another factor underlying the tension I often felt around women to whom I was attracted is the close connection between sexuality and spirituality. We are at once sexual and spiritual in our human nature. We need deep human connection to be fully alive, and we need a personal and intimate relationship to God to fulfill our deepest desires. If either need is frustrated or unmet, alienation follows. I believe that some people are called to celibacy but my experience teaches me it is a rare calling indeed.

Women generally open up emotionally to priests because they perceive priests as safe and trustworthy. As in the therapist-client relationship, women frequently fall in love with priests in whom they confide. Men are typically attracted by what they see with their eyes. I would at times find myself listening to an attractive women pouring her heart out about loneliness or alienation in her marriage and I would become aware of a strong physical attraction to her at which point I would shift my awareness back to the needs of the woman. I would tell myself that I was the professional and that although feelings of attraction are normal, I must not give in to that desire. Sometimes a woman would make it evident that she was interested in me emotionally and sexually, an energy I found to be flattering and enticing, the more so if I was feeling particularly lonely or needy.

I recall a mandatory meeting of all the priests of my diocese in which we were taught the absolute illegality of sexual involvement with a parishioner. We were told that we priests were the ones with the power so any violation of celibacy between a priest and parishioner was a violation of power and abuse of our authority. Although true in principle, my experience taught me that this principle leaves out a significant dynamic of a priest's life situation. Priests are often emotionally immature due to the very promise of celibacy which discourages priests from close relationships with women. Legally, the priests possess the power, but in fact, the woman is typically more emotionally and

sexually mature. That fact does not excuse priests' sexual involvement with women but it explains it in cases where the priest
possesses good will and intends to remain celibate.

Over the ensuing years, I gradually realized that mandatory
celibacy was an unhealthy lifestyle for most priests and bishops.
Studies reveal that over half of priests throughout the world do
not practice celibacy and are thus living double lives (see Richard
Sipe). Living with the secret of having a girlfriend or boyfriend
compromises the integrity of priests and bishops and severely un-
dermines the power of their preaching and the credibility of their
leadership. For clergy who do keep celibacy, many of them become neurotic which leads people to experience them as weird
or odd. Many priests try to satisfy their sexual urges by way of
masturbation and pornography.

I believe that there is a connection between celibacy and the
sexual abuse of minors. For priests who suffer from pedophilia,
i.e., men who are only attracted to prepubescent children, priestly celibacy offers a cover for their sickness. For priests who are
stuck at an adolescent level of psychosexual development, their
primary attraction will be to teenagers.

Many of my peers entered the seminary in the ninth grade
having never dated nor had the opportunity to learn to relate to
girls on a psychosexual level. The all male seminary and all male
clergy environment severely limit opportunities for maturing
through the stages of psychosexual development. Many priests
are leery of women because they perceive women as a threat to
chastity. Some priests are able to establish intimate friendships
with women without having sex but they are the exception. The
priests who shy away from friendships with women for fear of
sexual involvement too often remain quite immature in their
ability to relate to or interact with women. Consider the boy
who went through puberty in the seminary with little or no ex-
posure to girls. Twelve years later he is ordained a priest and finds

himself working around mostly women in church settings. The boy within him, still fearful of and awkward with girls, now as an adult finds himself distrustful of women which often manifests as coldness and anger towards them.

Negative attitudes among the clergy toward women and sex are deeply ingrained and often unconscious. Church leaders forbid even discussing changes to the celibate system because keeping the rule of celibacy going enables church leaders to maintain control over their clergy and their property assets. Calls for change are being raised more and more but resistance is strong and unbending.

One of the reasons I chose exile from priesthood in 2005 was that I could not in good conscience promote vocations to the priesthood due to the mandatory celibacy rule. Although I know some happy priests, I know very few who have the gift of celibacy and even fewer who actually practice it consistently. I recall a visiting missionary priest telling me that he had attended the ordination of a priest whose own father was the ordaining bishop. I asked the missionary why the Vatican allowed such hypocrisy and he answered that if the Vatican enforced the celibacy rule, there would be very few priests. The celibacy rule sets many priests up for failure and even death. I know of three gay priests in the Oakland Diocese who died of AIDS related causes. I know a gay pastor whose partner was present at his installation as pastor and who co-own a home.

The mandatory celibacy system is built on a myth and leads to rampant hypocrisy. This requirement is completely contrary to the workings of the Holy Spirit and leads to heartbreak and misery for priests, their partners, lovers, children, and many of the people they are called to serve. It took me years of personal struggle and witnessing the struggles of my brother priests to comprehend and accept that the Catholic Church was mandating such an unnatural and psychologically damaging practice.

I often weep within for the bishops and priests who go along with this destructive lie and cause harm to themselves and many other people in the process. The Catholic Church would enjoy far more competent and inspiring leadership if it would do away with mandatory celibacy. I applaud the pioneering work of Richard Sipe who has dedicated his life's work to studying celibacy and revealing how unhealthy a system it is for many Catholic priests and bishops. Only structural reform will get to the root of the celibacy problem by making celibacy optional.

Chapter Twenty-five

WOMEN

THE CATHOLIC CHURCH HIERARCHY'S VIEW of women is archaic and its policies discriminatory. What is it about women that Catholic leaders don't get? The recent excommunication of Maryknoll priest Roy Bourgeois for preaching at a women's ordination indicates the lengths to which Catholic officials will go to stifle dissent. Yet polls in the United States show that a majority of Catholics now favor women's ordination, but God help any bishop, priest or lay leader who publicly espouses such an opinion on this issue!

I recall taking a walk years ago with a close priest friend of mine when the topic of the role of women in the Church came up. My friend opined that he was not in favor of women's ordination because the priest represents Jesus at the altar and a woman could not adequately do that due to the gender difference. The fallacy of this reasoning is exposed by the fact that Jesus chose only Jews to be his Apostles yet Jewishness is not required for priestly ordination. I was incredulous that this contemporary of mine could actually believe that, yet he does! Centuries of tradition identifying God as male have left a strong resistance to women's ordination.

I think a large number of Catholics don't question the all male priesthood because that's all they have ever known, and because they have been conditioned not to question authority. They assume the Church leaders know best. My priest friend may have thought through the question and settled upon a rationale for keeping the status quo. Or he may have been unquestioningly parroting a long held justification for the prohibition of women's ordination.

Another priest who used to visit to dialog with me during my Sunday protests outside the Cathedral told me I was giving women false hope by advocating women's ordination because women can never be ordained. I asked him why, and he replied: " because two popes have taught definitively that women may never be ordained priests". That reply left me speechless but after I came to my senses, I spoke of my experience of women as being as smart and as capable as men, and as faith-filled as men. He agreed that women are gifted and capable but nevertheless, not called to priesthood. I said I thought women should have some say in such an exclusionary position at a time in history when women are running corporations and countries. This priest was not persuaded because he believes in the absolute authority of the Pope to decide who and who may not be ordained; case closed.

A woman taught religious education at my parish in Fremont. In one particular class on the sacraments, a little girl asked her how many sacraments there are. The teacher replied that there are seven for boys and six for girls. The little girl asked why girls could not be priests and her teacher had no rational answer to offer other than the truth: women have been excluded from ordination due to patriarchy, the view that men are intended by God to rule over women.

I recently read a book entitled THE ILLNESS THAT WE ARE, A JUNGIAN CRITIQUE OF CHRISTIANITY by John P. Dourly. A foundational premise of Jung's psychology argues "that psychic maturation, and so spiritual maturity too, can only take place through a relationship to the contrasexual energies both in the individual psyche and in other humans." (p. 61). When it comes to interpersonal relationships, particularly with women, my experience of my fellow priests in general is that they exhibit a high level of immaturity. I believe there is a direct correlation between our psychic immaturity and our lack of opportunity and permission for intimate relationships with women.

Karl Jung was fascinated by Catholic portrayals of the Virgin Mary. He believed that Catholic doctrines about Mary such as the Mother of God and the Assumption were an unconscious balancing of the Catholic tradition of reserving deity exclusively to the masculine. To quote Dourly's book, "If the Assumption means anything, it means a spiritual fact which can be formulated as the integration of the female principle into the Christian conception of the Godhead." (p. 60)

Pope John Paul II had many women friends but he was adamantly opposed to women's ordination and even forbade discussion of the topic. At the same time he spoke in defense of the equality of women and how man and woman complement one another.

During priest gatherings I used to be appalled by the absence of women. I thought how much more balanced and mature we would be with the presence of women as equals in our midst. I would recall all the women I know who are essentially doing the work of priests without benefit of ordination or title. The official resistance to women's ordination is a scandal to many women and men inside and outside the Catholic Church. During my last ten years in active priesthood, I used to speak openly and forcefully in favor of women's ordination. I found that many of my parishioners agreed with me as they wondered why in this day and age there continued to be any problem with the idea. Among the Spanish speaking parishioners, I found less support for women's ordination although I could sense that my arguments in favor were causing some to consider the possibility.

The principle argument used by the Vatican against women's ordination is that Jesus did not choose any women to be Apostles. The majority of Scripture scholars argue that this is not a valid argument against women's ordination. Another argument used by the Vatican is that the Church has never had women priests. That is not absolutely true, nor is it a valid argument for prohibiting women's ordination today. My priest friend was opposed to women's ordination because he believed Jesus' maleness was an essential requirement of the priest presider at a Catholic Mass. The other priest I mentioned argued against women's ordination on the basis of papal authority. As I reflect on the various arguments used to justify the status quo viz a viz women in the Church, I'm sensing something deeper here which remains largely unconscious: that is, a strong antipathy toward women based on the woman as temptress. A friend of mine wrote to me recently, "I am sad so many churches cling to misogyny leaving no place for me in them."

Observe how women religious have had to cover their bodies head to toe until quite recently. Notice how women in many Muslim countries cover their bodies to varying degrees. In the Catholic priesthood, men are required to renounce sexual relations with women and close friendships with women that might lead to sexual relations. Mary, the mother of Jesus, is declared ever-virgin by the Church even though the Gospels tell us Jesus had brothers and sisters. Pope John Paul often expressed his deep devotion to Mary and encouraged others, particularly priests, to devote themselves to her. Against this backdrop, the previously quoted John Dourly, a priest, writes: "A humanly unreal virgin and mother, when taken literally. . .can only contribute to hostility toward real women, and confirm the threat that women presumably pose to a masculine spirit in pursuit of a perfection defined in terms that virtually exclude a living relation to the feminine." (p. 61)

"Hostility toward real women" jumps off the page at me because I see that hostility towards women acted out by priests and other men again and again. Ask almost any woman who has worked for the Church and the stories will come flooding out, unless of course they feel their job is at stake. This situation of hostility towards women has been codified into church doctrine and practice and we are all the poorer for it. By 2004 when I decided to choose voluntary exile from the priesthood, I had reached a point where the institutionalized sexism of the Catholic Church was such a profound and scandalous injustice to me that I could no longer officially represent such an institution.

Even though women are excluded from the ranks of the hierarchy, I am heartened and inspired by many women leaders in the Church today, in particular Elizabeth A. Johnson, a theologian at Fordham University. Her 2008 book, QUEST FOR THE LIVING GOD, is one of the best theology books I have ever read. The last chapter is on the Trinity and makes a direct connection between our image of God and our ways of dealing with one another: "Deeply hurtful attitudes and practices have arisen in church and society because one group imagines itself superior to another. The resulting stratification of power, with some dominant, some subordinate, shapes institutions of racism, sexism, ecclesiastical clericalism, and ruination of the earth, among other pernicious sins. The revitalized idea of the Trinity makes clear that, far from existing as a monarch ruling from isolated splendor and lording it over others, the living God is an overflowing communion of self-giving love. The practical importance of this notion lies in the way it exposes the perversion of patriarchy, racism and other sinful patterns." (p. 223)

Since my decision for exile, the afore mentioned Fr. Roy Bourgeois, a well-known Maryknoll priest and justice activist, has been excommunicated (2008) and laicized (2012) for taking part in a women's ordination ceremony and for refusing to publicly renounce his oft stated belief that God is calling women, not just men, to the priesthood. Yet Church authorities have not excommunicated priest child abusers nor bishops who knowingly reassigned priest child abusers to other parishes. This lack of proportion between the punishment meted out to Fr. Roy Bourgeois on the one hand, and priest child abusers on the other boggles my mind.

However, it is Catholic women who suffer the greatest punishment. I weep within for all the women whose gifts are not being fully utilized by the Church and for all the women and girls who are treated like second class citizens just because of their gender. How noble and courageous are all the women and men who are speaking out against this injustice even at the risk of persecution and suffering. Women's time is coming in the Catholic Church because the Holy Spirit's voice can be stifled for only so long. Fr. Roy Bourgeois says it best: "The Vatican and Maryknoll can dismiss me, but they cannot dismiss the issue of gender equality in the Catholic Church. The demand for gender equality is rooted in justice and dignity will not go away." (Nov. 20, 2012 statement about his dismissal from Maryknoll) When gender equality happens, the Church, its priests and laity, will be so much better for it.

Chapter Twenty-six

SEXUAL ORIENTATION

No topic in my preaching experience brought up as much gut level emotional reaction as that of homosexuality. Surveys show that Americans' attitudes toward gay and lesbian people are changing fairly rapidly in the direction of acceptance. Not so in the world of popes and bishops. Official Church teaching stigmatizes the homosexual orientation as "intrinsically disordered." Pastoral teaching tries to moderate this harsh position by directing Catholics to love gay and lesbian people and not to discriminate on the basis of sexual orientation. It's as if the Church is saying to its gay and lesbian members: "You are freaks but we still love you. Just don't express your love sexually."

The Church's official position on homosexuality was another reason I chose exile from the priesthood but it took me years to see how unjust that position is. I had grown up breathing in the homophobia of my generation. I felt a little uncomfortable around effeminate men and masculine women. I accepted Church teaching that gay sex was unnatural and therefore sinful. At my twentieth high school reunion in 1987, I learned that a woman I'd attended a couple of school dances with had come out as a lesbian. After the reunion, I wrote her a letter gently criticizing her for identifying as lesbian. I could not at the time accept that she was attracted to women. In my letter I expressed my disappointment with her decision and tried to talk her out of it. I received no reply. Years later I wrote to apologize profusely. She graciously accepted my apology while letting me know how much my original letter hurt her emotionally.

What finally opened my eyes to my ignorance and prejudice were gay and lesbian people that I either knew personally through family, friends and parish, or people I had read about. I had begun to feel sympathy for gay men who were striving to remain celibate but routinely having sexual encounters. They told me of their guilt and loneliness and I felt compassion for them. I began to question the wisdom of Church teaching on this matter. I remember reading a piece by Andrew Sullivan years ago about what a struggle it was for him to be gay and Catholic. Sullivan, an accomplished English journalist working in the U.S., is devout, articulate, and deeply troubled by the Church's inability to accept his sexual orientation and humanity as a gift from God. Sullivan's pain and suffering, caused by the Church's rigid teaching made a big impact on me.

More recently a gay priest, Father Geoff Farrow, in October, 2008, while pastor of the Newman Center at Fresno State University, gave a powerful talk at Sunday Mass about why he could not comply with his bishop's order to direct parishioners to vote "Yes" on Proposition 8 (to outlaw same sex marriage). His talk is worth quoting at length:

> *In directing the faithful to vote "Yes" on Proposition 8,*
> *the California Bishops are not merely entering the political*
> *arena, they are ignoring the advances and insights of*
> *neurology, psychology and the very statements made by the*
> *Church that homosexuality is innate (i.e. orientation). In*
> *doing this, they are making a statement which has a direct,*
> *and damaging, effect on some of the people who may be*
> *sitting in the pews next to you today. The statement made by*
> *the bishop reaffirms the feelings of exclusion and alienation*

*that are suffered by individual loved ones who have left the
Church over this issue.*

*Imagine what hearing such damaging words at Mass
does to an adolescent who has just discovered that he/she
is gay/lesbian? What is the hierarchy saying to him/her?
What are they demanding from that individual? What
would it have meant to you personally to hear from the
pulpit at church that you could never date? Never fall in
love, never kiss or hold hands with another person? Never
be able to marry? How would you view yourself? How
would others hearing these words be directed to view you?
How would you view your life and your future? How
would you feel when you saw a car with a "Yes on 8"
bumper sticker, or when you overheard someone in a public
place use the word "faggot?"*

*In effect, the bishops are asking gay and lesbian people
to live their lives alone. . . How is marriage protected by
intimidating gay and lesbian people into loveless and
lonely lives. What is accomplished by this? Worse still, is
to intimidate a gay or lesbian person into a heterosexual
marriage, which is doomed from its inception, and makes
two victims instead of one by this hurtful 'theology'. This
'theology', which is parroted by clerics in polished tones from
pulpits, produces the very prejudice and hatred in our society
which they claim to abhor.*

*I know these words will cost me dearly. But to withhold
them, would be far more costly and I would become an
accomplice to moral evil that strips gay and lesbian people not
only of their civil rights but of their human dignity as well.*

What it cost Father Geoff Farrow was his job and livelihood.
He was removed from his position a few days after that October
5, 2008 talk.

Here in the Diocese of Oakland, many of the priests are gay but none openly. Some are sexually active, others not. Some are mature, some less so. Due to fear, most gay priests remain closeted and silent about gay issues Like many heterosexual priests, many gay priests are homophobic. I do not know the sexual orientation of former Bishop of Oakland Salvatore Cordileone but I do know that he puts a lot of time and energy into opposing gay marriage all under the guise of protecting heterosexual marriage. In his moral self righteousness, Bishop Cordileone lays heavy burdens upon gay and lesbian people. Priests who remain silent on gay issues are passive perpetuators of injustice.

Not everyone who opposes gay marriage is homophobic. Some are following what is taught by the Church and Scripture. In the June 15, 2007, issue of Commonweal Magazine, Luke Timothy Johnson presents his views on homosexuality under the theme of "Scripture and Experience". He cites several examples of how Church positions seemingly backed by the Bible have changed due to people's lived experience. One such issue is slavery. He says another is homosexuality. Here is Johnson in his own words:

> *Many of us who stand for the full recognition of gay*
> *and lesbian persons within the Christian communion*
> *find ourselves in a position similar to that of the early*
> *abolitionists—and of the early advocates for women's full*
> *and equal roles in church and society. We are fully aware of*
> *the weight of Scriptural evidence pointing away from our*
> *position, yet place our trust in the power of the living God*
> *to reveal as powerfully through personal experience and*
> *testimony as through written texts. To justify this trust, we*
> *invoke the basic Pauline principle that the Spirit gives life*
> *but the letter kills (2 Corinthians 3:6). And if the letter*
> *of Scripture cannot find room for the activity of the living*

God in the transformation of human lives, then trust and
obedience must be paid to the living God rather than to the
words of Scripture.

Jesus did not leave us answers or blueprints for how to deal with many modern day problems. What he did leave was the Holy Spirit to guide us in God's ways, and for us to follow the Spirit's guidance, we need to take our experience seriously by listening to people's stories. Gay and lesbian people's stories are as important for us to listen to as Scripture and Church teaching on the topic. God does reveal in Scripture but Scripture is a compendium of other people's experience. We do not follow every law in Scripture because the Spirit guides us in light of our lived lives today. In the Acts of the Apostles, Paul challenged Peter to be tolerant of gentiles wanting to join the Church even though Peter could quote Scripture at length to justify why gentiles should be circumcised and required to eat kosher foods. Peter had to struggle to fully accept gentiles into the Church and so too some of us have to struggle to understand and accept gay and lesbian people and their need to love and marry. Luke Timothy Johnson again:

I suggest, therefore, that the New Testament provides
impressive support for reliance on the experience of God in
human lives—not in its commands, but in its narratives and
in the very process by which it came into existence. In what
way are we to take seriously the authority of Scripture?
What I find most important of all is not the authority found
in specific commands, which are fallible, conflicting, and
often culturally conditioned, but rather the way Scripture
creates the mind of Christ in its readers, authorizing them
to reinterpret written texts in light of God's Holy Spirit
active in human lives. When read within the perspective of a
Scripture that speaks everywhere of a God disclosing Godself

through human experience, our stories become the medium of God's very revelation.

Recently I was protesting outside the Cathedral with Billy Bradford, a gay activist. A Bible preacher approached us and began telling us how homosexuality is an abomination and cited the book of Leviticus to back his point. Billy challenged the preacher by citing Leviticus' prohibition of eating shrimp and said he guessed that the preacher probably enjoyed eating shrimp from time to time. The Bible preacher was speechless for a moment as he thought about the shrimp argument. Billy's use of Scripture to argue against Scripture was clever and telling.

Homosexuality has been a controversial topic throughout most of history in most of the world. But in light of growing understanding and acceptance of gays and lesbians, those still opposing homosexuality as an abomination are digging in their heels even deeper even as their positions look more and more foolish. On the front page of the March 31, 2005, New York Times, the following headline appeared: CLERGY FIGHTING A GAY FESTIVAL FOR JERUSALEM. The story reported how religious leaders of Christianity, Islam, and Judaism were united against a planned gay pride festival because they said the "event would desecrate the city and convey the erroneous impression that homosexuality is acceptable." A Sufi sheik said, "We can't permit anybody to come and make the Holy City dirty. This is very ugly and very nasty to have these people come to Jerusalem." How ironic that all these religious leaders could unite against homosexuality when such issues as war and peace, the plight of Palestinians, and terrorism defied their finding any common ground. Later, the Pope lamented that the gay pride festival had been held describing it as "an offense to the Christian values of a city that is so dear to the hearts of Catholics across the world." An American rabbi vehemently opposed the festival calling it "the spiritual rape of the Holy City." He added, "This is not the homo land, this is the Holy Land."

Such intolerance, fear and hatred coming from the mouths of Christian, Muslim, and Jewish religious leaders indicates how deep-seated and passionate the opposition to homosexuality is throughout the world. In Jesus' time, he showed solidarity with lepers, women, the sick, the tax collectors, and the prostitutes, and for that he was put to death in Jerusalem. Although Jesus never mentioned homosexuality, his love for people on the margins and those being scapegoated makes clear to me how he would relate to gay and lesbians people today.

The Catholic Church should be leading the way to acceptance and understanding about homosexuality, but instead, many of its leaders are vilifying gay and lesbian people even as the ranks of the clergy are disproportionately filled with men of homosexual orientation. I saw this phenomenon up close and personal in the Diocese of Oakland. I feel deeply for my fellow priests who are gay because they are caught in a terrible predicament: to either defend Church teaching and policy or to follow the prophetic stand taken by Fr. Geoffrey Farrow. To date, no gay priests have taken a prophetic stand in this diocese.

No one chooses to be gay or lesbian. None of us chooses to whom we are attracted. The Spirit is drawing attention to the terrible prejudice and injustice suffered by gay and lesbian people often in the name of religion. The best pastor I worked with happened to be gay. He finally left the priesthood under the stress of having to keep an essential part of his humanity secret. Thankfully, this good man did not lose his faith but did find love in a committed relationship. Feeling unwelcome in the Catholic Church, my friend and his partner now practice their faith in an Episcopelian parish. I feel deep sadness that the Catholic Church remains so out of touch with the movement of the Spirit opening people's eyes to the dignity of gay and lesbian people and their love for each other. Only structural reform will get to the root of the problem of homophobia and exclusion in the Catholic Church. In this instance, structural reform would include a change in Catholic teaching and practice. Gay and lesbian people would no longer be stigmatized as disordered and gay marriage would be blessed and celebrated. Under the current system, the priests suffer, the people in the parishes suffer, and the mission of Jesus suffers.

Chapter Twenty-seven

THE SCANDAL MISSING FROM
THE HEADLINES

CLERICALISM, THE WIDELY HELD BELIEF that priests and bishops are superior to lay people, has caused a scandal which often goes unreported: the low standards set for parish priests and the resultant widespread unprofessional conduct. Some priests get away with appalling behavior and drive people away from the Church while the bishop looks the other way unless the misbehavior involves stealing parish money. In any other institution of its size and stature, pastors, who are equivalent to branch managers, would lose their jobs for such dereliction of duty, irresponsibility, rudeness, and gross incompetence. I am not referring here to criminal conduct such as sexual abuse of youth and children; I am referring to the way priests do their jobs.

In 1980, one year after my ordination, then Bishop of Oakland, John Cummins, invited my three classmates and me over to his residence in Oakland to see how we were doing in our still new ministry as parish priests. In the course of our visit, the Bishop asked us how things were going. I shared with him stories about a neighboring pastor I'd been hearing about from parishioners, Father John Morgan, the then notorious pastor of St. James Parish in Fremont. I told John Cummins that Fr. Morgan was known for angry outbursts and erratic behavior such as chasing a man off of parish property with his (Morgan's) car, with ordering the ushers to lock the doors of the church after Mass started so people couldn't walk into Mass late, and telling people at Mass not to put coins in the collection basket because that was a sign of cheapness; Fr. Morgan demanded only bills, no coins. Bishop Cummins replied to me in effect that we priests need to take better care of each other. Fr. Morgan remained in place for years, but that wasn't the end of the saga.

After our meeting with the Bishop, I was transferred to another part of the diocese and out of earshot of John Morgan's egregious behavior. Years later when I was assigned to Corpus Christi Parish in Fremont not far from Fr. Morgan's parish, I resumed hearing stories about his angry rude ways with parishioners. At a priests' convocation, the topic for discussion was clergy standards. In my small group, I shared with my fellow priests how I'd been hearing about Fr. Morgan's despicable behavior for years even though I'd alerted Bishop Cummins about him twenty years earlier. My colleagues chose me to be their spokesperson when we returned to the full gathering of priests and they encouraged me to tell the Morgan story. Morgan himself was not at the convocation because true to his curmudgeonly nature, he didn't attend such gatherings. When the time came for me to speak on behalf of our small group, I told the story of Fr. Morgan. You could have heard a pin drop in the hall because I was naming a troubled priest and doing so in the presence of the bishop who had left the priest in place to terrorize his parishioners for over twenty years. I was breaking a taboo: public criticism of a fellow cleric.

Thankfully, the priest who was head of the Personnel Board at the time brought my complaint up at their next meeting which led in turn to Bishop Cummins asking Fr. Morgan to retire. Why did it take so long? The same mentality, clericalism, which led Bishop Cummins and most other U.S. bishops to move abuser priests from parish to parish, is what kept Fr. Morgan in a position of authority and trust for decades.

Fr. Morgan's behavior was egregious but not unique. Another pastor in my corner of the diocese would take scores of vacations, sometimes not even letting his staff know where he was going. One Saturday afternoon, a couple showed up for a Mass to celebrate their long scheduled 50th wedding anniversary along with a large number of family and friends. The pastor, who had committed to preside at the Mass, was nowhere to be found. Eventually, another priest came to the rescue to preside at the couple's celebration. Imagine the embarrassment and anger of the family being left out to dry by their absentee pastor! I heard about it through a friend of mine who was employed at that parish.

I used to be available for Confessions every Saturday between 3:30 and 4:30 p.m. Now and then a group of Spanish speaking women would show up for Confession. One of them complained to me that the reason she came to my church for Confession was because her pastor often didn't show up at the time scheduled for Confessions.

A friend of mine in a neighboring parish quit going to church when his pastor started using funds donated to the St. Vincent de Paul ministry for the poor to pay parish bills. My friend complained to the pastor that this transfer of funds was immoral and dishonest, but to no avail.

Yet another neighboring pastor, known for being eccentric and prone to angry outbursts, once had a diabetic seizure during the noon Mass. Paramedics were called but when they tried to take this priest to the hospital, he screamed at them, created a big scene, and adamantly refused to be taken away. The priest won the argument.

Another priest in my area was known to refuse to do weddings for couples already living together. He insisted that they first split up even if they could not afford it. Other priests would ignore the Diocese's guidelines for the sacraments of matrimony and baptism. Others would marry couples who by Church law required annulments of previous marriages because it was simply too much work and hassle.

For many years I belonged to a priest support group. One of the priests in our group served in the Archdiocese of San Francisco across the Bay. His pastor, who was accountable to no one, was upset with my friend for challenging him on various egregious practices. The Archbishop at the time, John Quinn, decided to transfer my friend. Our support group decided to go to bat for our friend so we arranged a meeting with the Archbishop. We complained to Quinn that we thought it unfair of him to move our friend when it was the pastor who should have been disciplined. The Archbishop expressed sympathy for our position but said he felt his hands were tied. He had already had to retire several alcoholic pastors but didn't feel he could move our friend's pastor. Again, clericalism trumped justice.

The Second Vatican Council (1962-1965) taught that the number one ministry of the parish priest is preaching the Word of God, yet one of the biggest complaints one hears from Catholics is about the poor quality of preaching in their parishes. The most common complaints are "boring", "too long", "too political", and "too repetitive". Catholic preachers too often simply talk about the Bible readings instead of applying the message of the Scriptures to life. A good homily takes time to prepare, so many priests don't devote the necessary time and energy required. The telltale sign that a homily is going nowhere is when the priest begins it with, "In the first reading". . . The problem rests in part in the lack of adequate training in homiletics (the art of preaching) but more so in the fact that priests aren't making preaching a priority in their weekly schedule. Too many priests wing it. Others resort to homily services which offer prepared homilies for a subscription fee. These homilies tend to be bland, generic and disconnected from the lives of the parishioners hearing them and the priest reading them. The power of the preached word is subverted and the people go home unnourished. Poor preaching and dead liturgies drive some people away from the Church altogether. This is a scandal that does not make the headlines. A widely circulated quote attributed to Fr. Eugene Walsh, a noted liturgist, goes: "Good liturgy increases and strengthens faith; bad liturgy weakens and destroys faith".

Priests in large parishes are chronically busy. If you ask most of them how they are doing, they will inevitably tell you they are busy and weary. One such priest, a friend of mine, would schedule his evening appointments for every half hour. When I asked him if thirty minutes was sufficient time to deal with a serious life issue, he replied that he just didn't have the luxury to give people more time. I suggested we needed to address the priest shortage but he just sighed and said he didn't have time.

As the priest shortage has grown, the workload of priests has increased. Parishes which used to have three priests now have two, and ones with two now have one. Many parishes have no priest at all. I recall an article in America Magazine several years ago entitled "One Hundred Journeys". The author, a priest, travelled around the country preaching in parishes all over the U.S. to raise funds for the poor. Here are a few of his observations:

What have I seen? I doubt that I have seen a priest who was not strung-out in some way, over-extended by various and numerous demands, many rather trivial, few pertaining to the word and sacrament for which he was ordained. I have seen the priest without a satisfying community or social life, aloneness and loneliness tearing down human fibre, often without the lifegiving habits of proper nourishment, exercise and good housekeeping.

Few, very few, receive the encouragement and support they desire, perhaps inappropriately, from their bishops. Their morale is low. Their standing in the community is low. Where the clouds of pedophilia hang heavily, in places as distant from one another as Maine is from Louisiana, I have been asked not to wear a Roman collar in the local restaurant. The priests see little relief coming from the seminaries, not simply because vocations are few in number, but more so because they speak, if not of a homosexual clergy, then of an effeminate male clergy soon to be ordained.

Having experienced feeling lonely and chronically weary from overwork and stress, I feel compassion for my fellow priests. They are caught up in a system they feel powerless to change. So it is no surprise that some become negligent, irresponsible, absent, and bitter. A friend of mine knew he was becoming bitter and angry so he finally chose to leave the priesthood rather than repeatedly lose his temper with parishioners.

In most U.S. dioceses, foreign priests have been brought in as a solution to the shortage of American priests. Some of these priests lack command of the English language; most lack an understanding of U.S. culture. Some come to the U.S. for the wrong reasons such as escaping problems at home or to better their lifestyle. I have often heard from Catholic friends that their foreign priest means well but his English is too hard to understand.

I worked with a priest from India who spoke many languages including Spanish. He would sometimes celebrate the Spanish Mass on Sunday. One time a Mexican woman asked him to please speak more slowly so as to be understood. The priest berated her for criticizing his Spanish and told her that his Spanish was far superior to hers.

I brought my concerns about priest professional standards directly to Bishops Cummins and Vigneron. Both acknowledged that things could always be better but that we live in an imperfect world. Neither did anything to use their considerable authority to address the specific problems I brought to their attention. Both seemed fearful of confrontation and neither appeared concerned about the pain and suffering being inflicted on the people under the authority of incompetent or irresponsible pastors. I used to have great expectations that bishops would use their authority to build up the Church. Now I have no expectations of bishops because I have seen them put the welfare of priests ahead of parishioners over and over again, and to act concerned about clergy sexual abuse only when the press or the courts bring the scandal into the light of public consciousness. Gary Wills writes that the bishops have become "boring and irrelevant" and to a point he's right, except that by their action and inaction, many people are still being harmed. The people need and deserve better leaders both at the parish and diocesan level.

The current policy of the Church to only ordain single men is out of step with the signs of the times and keeps the Holy Spirit from calling forth competent and inspirational preachers and pastors for the local parish communities. Countless gifted women and married men are excluded from ordination based solely on rigid adherence to Church tradition. Meanwhile the priests who are in place are tired, cranky, and overwhelmed. Many compensate for their weariness and loneliness in unhealthy ways. Parishioners are leaving the Church in droves because they are not being nourished by their shepherds.

Bishops have a responsibility to provide good shepherds for every parish and would do well to heed the words of Ezekiel the prophet:

*Thus says the Lord God: Woe to the shepherds of Israel who
have been pasturing themselves! Should not shepherds, rather,
pasture sheep? You have fed off their milk, worn their wool,
and slaughtered their fatlings, but the sheep you have not
pastured. You did not strengthen the weak nor heal the sick
nor bind up the injured. You did not bring back the strayed
nor seek the lost, but you lorded it over them harshly and
brutally. So they were scattered for lack of a shepherd, and
became food for all the wild beasts. . .*

   *Therefore, shepherds, hear the word of the Lord: As I
live, says the Lord god, because my sheep have been given
over to pillage, and because my sheep have become food for
every wild beast, for lack of a shepherd; because my shepherds
did not look after my sheep, but pastured themselves and did
not pasture my sheep; because of this, shepherds hear the
word of the Lord: Thus says the Lord God: I swear I am
coming against these shepherds. I will claim my sheep from
them and put a stop to their shepherding my sheep so that
they may no longer pasture themselves. I will save my sheep,
that they may no longer be food for their mouths.*
(EZEKIEL 34, 2-10)

These words apply equally to bishops who fail to remove sexually abusive priests from ministry and to priests who abuse, and to
the scandal missing from the headlines: the increasing number of
incompetent, irresponsible and immoral pastors of parishes.

   I dream of the day when every parish will have a good shepherd, male or female, married or single, gay or straight: a pastor who loves Jesus, loves him or herself, and loves the people,
preaches competently, and shows up when expected, who knows
how to build community and is humble enough to accept criticism. The quality of priestly ministry is very poor at the moment and there are no signs that it will improve in the future.

Only structural reform will get to the root of the problem of low standards for clergy leaders. Under the present structure, priests are set up for failure by lack of support, companionship, and accountability. The priests who fail at their job are many. Some should never have been ordained in the first place while only a few are extremely gifted and faith-filled. This scandal behind the scandal is a symptom of a failed system and its primary victims are the people in the pews each Sunday, and those others who just walk away frustrated, angry, or bored.

Chapter Twenty-eight
FALLEN HEROES

THE CHURCH HAS BEEN DEEPLY WOUNDED by the sexual abuse of children and youth by priests and bishops. It is also wounded by the fall of thousands of priests across the United States and world. This wound extends to parishioners, family and friends, and calls for grieving and structural reform. I have been scandalized countless times by priests who have violated the trust of children and teenagers. Some of these criminal priests were once my heroes and their falls from grace brought me feelings of disillusionment, sadness, anger, and betrayal. If these gifted men could fail so miserably, what priest is immune to a similar fate?

My earliest priest heroes were parish priests whose preaching enkindled in me a desire to seek God and live the Gospel in the spirit of Jesus. Fr. Rogan at Blessed Sacrament Parish in Washington, D.C. and Msgr. Burke at St. Thomas More Parish in Arlington, Virginia, come to mind. Their preaching at Sunday Mass was inspiring and struck me as profoundly true. I dreaded it when other priests gave the homily because they tended to be boring, repetitive, and long winded. After I entered the seminary, I looked up to Dick Basso, Bob Gavin, and other faculty members whose preaching, teaching and example provided me role models to emulate.

After ordination I looked up to priests in my diocese such as George Crespin, Brian Joyce, Dan Danielson and Richard

Mangini, all post Vatican II priests who were dedicated to building up the Church by serving people with love, compassion and humility. Priests outside my diocese who captured my respect and admiration were Fr. Bruce Ritter, founder of Covenant House, John Powell, S.J., psychologist and best-selling author, Vince Dwyer, Thomas Merton, Henri Nouwen and Dale Fushek, founder of Life Teen. All of these men were accomplished leaders. As I followed their careers for inspiration and role modeling, I was wounded by some of them when their statues, erected by me, fell off their pedestals onto me. One of the reasons so many Catholics remain in denial about clergy sexual abuse is that these moral failures and criminal acts are in such stark contrast to the public image of much admired priests.

Friends of mine in the Diocese of Stockton have been friends for years with a priest name Michael Kelly. He was accused of molesting an altar boy twenty-five years ago. Due to the statute of limitations, Kelly could not be criminally prosecuted but he was tried civilly and found guilty. Many of his parishioners continued to declare his innocence. Before the judge declared the penalties, Fr. Kelly returned to Ireland stressing bad health as the reason. He has since been accused by two other adults. My friends cannot imagine how he could be guilty of such offenses. I understand and sympathize with their pain and disbelief. I also have gently explained to them that child abusers are masters of deception.

During my first year in the graduate level seminary, three priest faculty members left the priesthood, and ones of them, Fr. Jack, happened to be my spiritual director. I learned of Jack's departure not from Jack but from the seminary rector who announced it during our first community Mass after Christmas break. I was shocked and saddened and wondered how and why this could be. Jack was an excellent teacher and a competent spiritual director. The reason for Jack's leaving was not given at the time but I learned later that he left the priesthood to marry a woman with whom he had been involved for some time. I should not have been surprised by Jack's decision, after all, thousands of priests left to marry during the late 60's and beyond, but I had unfairly judged them as commitment breakers who did not take their vows seriously. How judgmental I was! I noticed that once a priest left the priesthood, one rarely heard his name mentioned again, and these men were certainly not invited back to say goodbye. The silence was loud and carried a strong message: a priest who leaves is "persona non grata". Some of my fellow students seemed to take the faculty members' leaving more in stride because they had been in the seminary system longer and seen others leave before. Meanwhile, I was left feeling devastated. .But Jack was only the first of many fallen heroes, and in hindsight, Jack's reason for leaving looks healthy. I would soon painfully learn of many priests who were much less psychosexually mature than Jack, men who betrayed their vocation by sexual assaults on children and teens.

One such priest was Fr. Bruce Ritter, a Franciscan, who founded an organization called Covenant House in New York City in 1972. He had been teaching at Manhattan College when he became aware of runaway teens in the area. His students challenged him to do something for these endangered and needy teens, so he did. Covenant House offered shelter, counseling, and rehab services to teens. Fr. Bruce was a powerful spokesperson for a great cause that that grew by leaps and bounds into a national and then international organization. I heard him on tape telling the story of how and why he started this effective outreach to homeless teens, an appeal which inspired me to begin sending Covenant House regular donations. Fr. Bruce was articulate and inspirational. Covenant House grew like wildfire because of a real need and also because of Bruce Ritter's leadership.

When the fall came, it came hard and fast. Bruce Ritter was sexually abusing some of the runaway teens in his program and using donations to help out his own family members. I couldn't believe it, at first. How could this happen! What a price we pay for the repression of sexual desire, and how right Jesus is about the dangers of money! Covenant House still exists but one rarely hears about it anymore. I find it hard to trust celibates who spend their time serving the needs of teens and children. I even wonder about certain saints who founded religious orders to care for kids, and my distrust includes female saints as well.

Fr. John Powell was a Jesuit priest out of Chicago who became well known for his many books, tapes, and lectures on love and relationships. I have read all his books at least once and some of them twice. I have quoted John Powell in homilies and used his video and tape series with adult education groups in parishes. Certainly this was one priest worthy of trust: charismatic, humble, wise, compassionate, faith-filled, and an expert in relationships. But lo and behold, it became known that Fr. John Powell had sexually abused at least seven teenage girls in the 1960's and 1970's leading to many lawsuits. John Powell dropped off the face of the earth and out of my pantheon of priest heroes and died in 2009. His public fall seemed completely incongruous with his writings and public persona. I felt tremendous sadness and consternation when I first learned of Powell's crimes.

Fr. Vince Dwyer was a Trappist (Cistertian) priest who for health reasons had to abandon the monastic life. He developed a ministry to priests around the country teaching them how to adapt to the reforms of Vatican II. He spoke to us priests of the Diocese of Oakland sometime in the 1980's and made a deeply positive impression. I took copious notes and later devoured his book. LIFT YOUR SAILS: THE CHALLENGE OF BEING A CHRISTIAN.

But Fr. Vince Dwyer had a shadow side that manifested itself in a long-term sexual relationship with a high school student beginning when she was 15 until she was 28. The Trappists paid the woman a settlement and swore her to silence but she told her painful story publicly in 2002. In 1998, a male who had been a seminarian under Dwyer's authority, made an accusation against him too. Vince Dwyer was released from the Trappist order and has dropped out of sight. What a tragedy for his victims, for him, and for all who like me found inspiration from his motivational talks and from his book.

Fr. Dale Fushek was pastor of St. Timothy Parish in Mesa, Arizona, when he founded Life Teen, a world-wide teen program which I described in chapter six. Fr. Dale was extremely charismatic and persuasive. Both teens and adults were drawn to him as a person and to the way he communicated Christian faith to teenagers. But in late 2005 Fushek was arrested and charged with fondling boys in his parish and asking them prying questions about their sex lives between 1984 and 1994. Fushek had resigned as pastor in April, 2005, when someone claimed to have recovered a respressed memory involving sexual improprieties by the priest in 1985. Fushek had also served as vicar general of the Phoenix Archdiocese, the second highest official next to the Archbishop. Fushek avoided jail, left the priesthood and the Catholic Church to found his own church.

Closer to home, it was revealed that Fr. George Crespin and Fr. Brian Joyce of the Diocese of Oakland, while working as assistants to Bishops Begin and Cummins, had knowingly gone along with allowing known sexual abuser priests to remain in ministry with access to kids. George Crespin was himself accused of abuse of a teenager. He denied the charge but the Diocese paid over $600,000 to his accuser as part of a $60,000,000 group settlement in 2005. I wrote to George asking him why, if innocent, he did not go to trial with his accuser. I received no response. Crespin and Joyce are both progressive and pastorally competent pastors. I felt disillusioned when I learned of their misdeeds.

World renowned Catholic priest authors Thomas Merton and Henri Nouwen both struggled with celibate loneliness. Merton's journals, published posthumously, tell of his affair with a nurse, a relationship that brought him great joy. Nouwen was a gay man whose broken relationship with another man sent him into a deep depression from which he eventually emerged.

I share these stories not to point out that priests have feet of clay, but to indicate how the celibate system brings even the most gifted and knowledgeable of priests to at best, the violation of promises and vows, and at worst, the commission of serious crimes. May their stories not be told in vain; rather may they lead the Catholic Church to embark in the urgent quest for structural reform for the sake of children, teenagers, adults, priests, bishops and the entire Body of Christ.

Chapter Twenty-nine
THE CHURCH AS IDOL

I FIND IT BOTH ENCOURAGING AND DAUNTING that Jesus saved his strongest criticism for religious leaders. Being no stranger to hypocrisy myself, I cringe sometimes when Jesus is blasting the scribes and the Pharisees for theirs. Now that I am no longer an active religious leader and find little to admire in most of the ones still active, I am encouraged by Jesus' stern warnings to religious leaders to exercise their authority humbly with an eye on service, not on reputation, privilege, money or rank.

In previous chapters, I have recounted numerous examples of the abuse of authority by priests and bishops. I have also spoken of my efforts to challenge bishops and priests at times when they have abused their authority. One of the walls I and other reform-minded people run into is our being told that we should be obedient to church authority, or specifically to the magisterium, the Latin rooted term for the teaching authority of the Pope and bishops. The assumption behind this argument is that God through Jesus to Peter and his successors has given ultimate authority to the Pope and bishops. For those who hold this position, the litmus test for being a true and orthodox Catholic is obedience to the magisterium. Those who are not absolutely or blindly obedient are considered dissenters and thus unorthodox.

Because I am refusing an assignment from my bishop here in Oakland, I am considered by some to be a dissenting priest who is being disobedient to the magisterium. What is lost in this view of church authority are more basic questions about Gospel values, about reading the signs of the times, about dialogue, about the sense of the faithful (what the people in the pews believe and hold as true teaching), about Jesus and the Holy Spirit.

When the magisterium is treated as an absolute value and ultimate authority without accountability to the Gospel and the people in the pews, the Church becomes an idol in place of God, and the Church loses its way, which is precisely what has happened. I remember reading an article about the title "Vicar of Christ" which is often used of the Pope. The author argued that the Pope is not the Vicar of Christ but the Vicar of Peter. A vicar is one who stands in the place of. The Pope represents Peter, the chief Apostle, not Christ. The Vicar of Christ on earth is the Holy Spirit. It may seem a small point made over words but the papal title Vicar of Christ is a symptom of the idolatry of placing the church on the level of God. The problem does not lie with the legitimate authority of Pope and bishops in Catholic tradition but in making an idol of that authority, an authority without real accountability. The Lay Review Board appointed by the U.S. Catholic bishops in 2003 wrote: "The exercise of authority without accountability is not servant leadership. It is tyranny." (as quoted in GOOD CATHOLIC GIRLS by Angela Bonavoglia, p. 72).

When a fellow priest said I had no right to advocate for the ordination of women, he did so on the basis of the "definitive teaching" of two recent popes on the matter. Church authority is too often used as a sledge hammer that is its own justification. A former bishop of Insbruck, Austria, at age 75 just before his retirement in 1998, criticized the Church on just this issue of how it uses and views its authority:

> *This is the real reason for the decline in papal authority.*
> *This authority, which is vitally necessary for the church,*

derives its force from agreement with Christ—as we see in
the case of papal infallibility. History shows, however, that
in practice even the church's highest officeholder can stray
from Christ.

As things now stand, Rome has lost the image of mercy
and assumed the image of harsh authority. . .We cannot have
a church in which those in the highest positions worry about
every speck in the eyes of people at the grassroots but not at
all about the plank in their own.
(NATIONAL CATHOLIC REPORTER, 12/26/1997/1/2/1998, P. 28)

Garry Wills, historian and author, in his book PAPAL SIN,
STRUCTURES OF DECEIT, criticizes the modern papacy
for its lack of intellectual honesty. In a 2000 review of the
book by John L. Allen Jr. in the National Catholic Reporter,
Allen writes:

Because the papal system is incapable of acknowledging error,
Wills believes, it drives apologists into mental gymnastics to
defend doctrines for which there are no good arguments. For
example, women were barred from the Catholic priesthood
because of antique beliefs about ritual impurity and
masculine superiority. Since it is no longer possible to invoke
those principles, defenders of the ban today are forced to claim
that because Jesus did not ordain women, the church cannot,
an assertion that even conservative Biblical scholars reject
on the grounds that the historical Jesus had no concept of
founding a priesthood, let alone excluding women from it.
(NCR, MAY 26, 2000, P. 13)

Thomas Cahill, author and historian, wrote a critique of
Pope John Paul II in the April 5, 2005 edition of the New York
Times in which he commented on this pope's legacy:

> . . .John Paul II's most lasting legacy to Catholicism will
> come from the episcopal appointments he made. In order
> to have been named a bishop, a priest must have been seen
> to be absolutely opposed to masturbation, pre-marital sex,
> birth control (including condoms used to prevent the spread
> of AIDS), abortion, divorce, homosexual relations, married
> priests, female priests and any hint of Marxism. It is nearly
> impossible to find men who subscribe whole-heartedly to
> this entire catalogue of certitudes; as a result the ranks of the
> episcopate are filled with mindless sycophants and intellectual
> incompetents. The good priests have been passed over; and
> not a few, in their growing frustration as the pontificate of
> John Paul Paul II stretched on, left the priesthood to seek
> fulfillment elsewhere.

Pope Paul VI went against the unanimous advice of the birth control commission the pope convened in the late 1960's because, he later admitted, he did not want to go against the consistent ban on artificial contraception imposed by his papal predecessors. Andrew Greeley found that Pope Paul VI"s encyclical "Humanae Vitae" drove more people away from the Church than any other single event in the 20th century. The Pope chose protecting the reputation of his fellow popes over the human need of his flock for effective means of family planning.

This recurring tendency of popes to choose tradition over human need is a symptom of the sin of idolatry wherein the Church takes the place of God. The head of the Church is Jesus, not the Pope (see Colossians 1, 18), but periodically in history, the Church forgets this fact and acts as if it knows better than God. Ending this idolatry is yet one more reason why the Church desperately needs structural reform. The Pope and bishops would benefit from the presence of women in their ranks, accountability for their behavior, and enough humility to admit past mistakes.

Chapter Thirty
DISSENT

REMEMBER THE BUMPER STICKER, "My Country Right or Wrong"? This sentiment expresses a false patriotism and assumes it is always wrong to question one's country. In the Church, there is a similar attitude, held by a vocal minority, that to question the decisions of the Pope and bishops is always wrong. Those who question the way the clergy sexual abuse crisis is being handled are called dissenters. The same goes for those who protest Church teachings on the role of women, gay and lesbian people, birth control, and many other issues. They are all dissenters and dissent cannot be tolerated by many in Church leadership and some of the laity as well.

If dissent was always wrong, we would all be following the Mosaic Law including kosher dietary rules. St. Paul dissented to St. Peter when Peter wanted to require Gentile Christians to be circumcised and eat kosher foods as reported in the Acts of the Apostles. In ACTS 15, 7, we read: "After much debate had taken place". . . among the Apostles and presbyters. Debate was thus expected in the early Church, as a means of decision making and a sign of the democratic nature of leadership in the first century of Christianity. That contrasts sharply with modern day Church leaders who remind those under their authority that "the Church is not a democracy". They are right in the sense that the Church does not constitute a democracy in the way a nation-state might, but the Church is democratic in nature when it respects the gift of the Holy Spirit in each of its members.

Many saints and prophets down the ages have dissented from church practices and teachings they considered contrary to God's will. Dissent is not always a bad thing; in fact, dissent is sometimes a necessary corrective, inspired by the Holy Spirit, to keep the Church in sync with the will of God. The current practice of Church authorities of refusing discussion of controversial issues such as women's ordination is a betrayal of God's gift of the Holy Spirit to all the baptized.

I encountered a few parishioners in every parish in which I served who questioned my right to dissent, i.e., to question Church authorities. I politely pointed out that the Holy Spirit is given to all the baptized and that popes and bishops do not have a monopoly on truth. Church history is replete with examples of false teaching by popes and bishops. Pope Boniface VIII taught that there is no salvation outside the Catholic Church. Thank goodness for the Spirit- led believers who dissented from that false teaching/heresy from the lips of a pope. Pope Paul VI in 1968 reaffirmed the Church ban on artificial birth control over against the recommendations of a broad section of Catholic clergy and laity to overturn the ban. As a result, the great majority of Catholics ignore the ban and use artificial birth control. Sadly, large numbers of Catholics have left the Church because of Pope Paul's egregious error in judgment.

I mentioned above that it is often said that the Church is not a democracy, usually in the context of criticism of dissenters. At present, the Church is a monarchy wherein the Pope, acting like a king, possesses absolute authority. What a terrible distortion of the legacy of Jesus who in choosing Peter to be leader of the Apostles stressed repeatedly the call to service. He washed Peter's feet to make the point but Peter did not appreciate it, at first.

The Church, if it to be true to Jesus, should look much more democratic than it does today. When God confers the Holy Spirit on believers through the sacraments of baptism and confirmation, God is empowering each member of the Church to speak and act in the Spirit for the good of all. Sometimes the Spirit moves Church members to dissent for the good of all.

The word "dissent" itself has become so associated with sinful disobedience that we need to find a word or phrase to capture the rightful role of respectful disagreement. Respectful disagreement is healthy, holy and human. What is not healthy, holy and human is for those in authority to prohibit respectful disagreement or to assume anyone who disagrees with a given Church policy and teaching is unorthodox or unfaithful.

After I expressed respectful disagreement to Bishop Vigneron in 2005 on Church policies regarding clergy sexual abuse, women and gay people, he told me that he would not engage in public debate even though he knew people would still talk about these issues. In other words, he was stifling dialogue because the Pope and bishops had imposed a gag order. Gag orders are not congruent with a Church docile to the Holy Spirit. Gag orders are used by leaders afraid of the truth from below.

The retired pope and most bishops are threatened by respectful disagreement because they are conditioned to believe they have a monopoly on truth and fidelity to authentic tradition. Bishop Vigneron told me that he would pray for me, implying that he would pray for me to see the error of my ways. I wrote to him suggesting he take off his Roman collar and pectoral cross (symbol of a bishop's authority) and listen to people who are feeling excluded by Church policies. There is no evidence he has done so.

Not only do the Pope and majority of bishops prohibit respectful disagreement but they often punish those who publicly disagree with Church teachings they arbitrarily determine to be sacrosanct. Before becoming the Pope Benedict XVI, Joseph Ratzinger gained the nickname "God's Rotweiler" for his ruthless suppression of dissent from theologians like Charles Curran, Leonardo Boff and over one hundred others. The Vatican of late has been launching investigations against nuns, the Girl Scouts, and theologians who respectfully question Church teachings. Catholic colleges are warned not to allow speakers who disagree with Church teaching but usually only teaching that has to do with abortion and sexual morality. As a result, an atmosphere of fear has been fostered at all levels of the Church at the same time that the Popes John Paul II and Benedict XVI and bishops have lost credibility for their egregious mishandling of the sexual abuse crisis.

I qualify as a "dissenter" now that I have refused a parish assignment because of the Oakland bishop's refusal to publicly dialogue about clergy sexual abuse, married clergy and women's ordination. I miss using my gifts of preaching, teaching and community building but feel that I am in good company with many others around the world who refuse to cooperate with Church leaders who try to silence respectful disagreement and ostracize those who advocate structural reform. Jesus' strongest criticism was directed against the religious leaders of his day, the scribes and Pharisees of first century Judaism (see Matthew 23). Sadly, that lesson has been lost on today's Church leaders.

Chapter Thirty-one

DENIAL, DENIAL, DENIAL

IN APRIL, 2012, I VISITED Santa Barbara, California, to attend the memorial of a friend. Being back in Santa Barbara brought to mind a visit years earlier to Mission Santa Barbara with a priest friend. On that visit we had stayed at the historic and scenic Mission and enjoyed a spirited game of tennis behind the church on the grounds of the now closed high school seminary. We felt nothing but gratitude towards our Franciscan hosts.

While back in Santa Barbara for the memorial service, I decided to revisit the Mission late on a beautiful Saturday spring afternoon since it was only about a mile walk up the hill from my motel. As I rounded the corner approaching the Mission, I was struck by the beauty of the place and the city park across the street from the church with its lovely rose garden and enormous lawn. As I approached the church for a visit, people were streaming out the front doors after a just concluded Mass. I walked up the scenic and historic steps hoping to take a look inside the church. The priest who had presided at the Mass was saying goodbye to Mass-goers as I approached. A woman trying to enter ahead of me was stopped by the priest from entering. He politely told her that the church doors were about to be closed for the evening and therefore she could not go in.

As I retreated back down the steps, I felt disappointed at not being able to enter the historic church but that feeling was dwarfed by a stronger emotion, a combination of irony and grief aroused in me by my keen awareness that this beautiful place of worship was adjacent to the former high school seminary where for decades scores of Franciscan priests and brothers abused scores of high school age boys. The Franciscan Order is still in litigation with abuse survivors and has resisted transparency about this sordid chapter of their history in 20th century California.

Did the people leaving Mass that day know about that history? Did they know that the Franciscan priest greeting them and preaching to them was a representative of a religious order that systematically abused male youth and covered up these heinous crimes until courageous abuse survivors forced their dark deeds into the light with the aid of lawyers, judges and news media? Did these Mass-going Catholics want to know the truth? Did they care that their offerings to the collection baskets during that Mass were helping pay lawyers deny justice to damaged-for-life abuse survivors?

I left the Mission church that beautiful spring afternoon with a heavy heart divided by my love for the Franciscans, the Mission, the people of God, and the rich Catholic tradition on the one hand, and the horrific crimes and cover-up by the Franciscan Order founded by one of my favorite saints, Francis of Assisi, on the other. I felt the pain of exile like never before and grieved for the crimes of my Church's leaders.

I have read that when people are exposed to terrible suffering or injustice over which they have no control, they learn to ignore it and carry on with life as best they can. This type of reaction seems to fit the behavior of most practicing Catholics today including, I imagine, the Mass-goers exiting Mission Santa Barbara on that April day. In democracies, citizens have the option of voting for or against candidates and policies to bring about change. In the Catholic Church, not only do people feel powerless to effect change but they have been trained to be passive, obedient followers of their ordained leaders. And so most practicing Catholics learn to put the corruption and abuse out of their minds so as to feel a certain level of comfort with attending Sunday Mass and supporting their parish financially. In the spirit of denial, they may tell themselves that the scandals in the Church do not apply to their parish priests or their diocesan bishop. The price people pay for denial is huge because it allows the secret celibate system to maintain itself and to use parish donations to secretly channel funds to pay for lawyers to deny abuse survivors justice and truth.

Everything seemed fine that sunny afternoon at the Santa Barbara Mission until I allowed myself the pain of remembering the true picture behind the scenic facade. My experience in Santa Barbara is one tiny snapshot of the denial that eats away at the Church's integrity throughout the world. All is not well with the Franciscans, with the Catholic bishops, and with the people who choose denial over solidarity with the victims of a very dangerous system of Church governance. This is not to say that all practicing Catholics are in denial. People continue to practice their faith for good reasons even as they abhor Church leaders who block meaningful reforms. The cover has been torn off the pretty package and its unpleasant contents are exposed for all to see. People of faith for whom their parish is their spiritual home are faced with agonizing choices for how to deal with the crisis. Nevertheless, denial continues to play a significant role in propping up an exposed and weakened leadership.

Part V

THE WAY FORWARD

Chapter Thirty-two
IMAGINING A HEALTHIER CHURCH

PEOPLE ASK ME IF I WILL EVER RETURN to active priesthood. I respond that it is extremely unlikely because I could never work in the present system, and the present system seems so entrenched that it's not likely to change much in my lifetime. Nevertheless, I do not underestimate the power of God, i.e., the Holy Spirit working in the world and the Church to bring about truth, love and justice. With Jesus' resurrection from the dead and the coming of the Holy Spirit, the war against falsehood and injustice has been won; the battle, however rages on. The way forward is Jesus, the way of truth, the way of death leading to resurrection. One of the early names for Christianity was "the way", and Jesus repeatedly stressed that it was not an easy or painless way.

The Church will never be completely free of sin until the return of Jesus in glory. In the meantime, what might the Church look like after the structural change I've been advocating throughout this book?

Some years ago, the Diocese of Oakland developed a document entitled "The Ten Essentials of Parish Life." These ten essentials were characteristics of a healthy and effective parish. I loved the process and the product except for one glaring omission among the essentials: the key role of the pastor in the life of the parish. Every study of parish life I've seen stresses how essential it is to have a competent pastor. The "Ten Essentials" omitted the leadership of a competent pastor because to include it would have led people to ask questions of their pastor and bishop which Church leaders were not prepared to entertain. The structural change now desperately needed in the Catholic Church cannot afford to ignore the leadership question. Jesus spent three years with his closest disciples training them to be leaders open to God, dependent on God, and fully aware of the price they would have to pay as servant leaders. An essential of parish life and church life is leadership, and leadership is what is most sorely lacking now in the Church at every level: the parish, the diocese, and the central administration at the Vatican.

A hallmark of Catholic tradition is the role of the Pope as the central leader of the Church in the tradition of Peter as chief apostle. Under the current structure, the Pope is not accountable to higher human authority because the rules give him absolute authority in decision-making. Vatican II tried to resurrect a tradition of the Pope as "first among equals" by stressing the collegial authority of the college of bishops and the autonomy of each bishop in his own diocese. But the Vatican Council still maintained the ultimate authority of the Pope. When the bishops gather in Rome for synods, the Pope sets the agenda and dictates the process, and also has final say over what decisions are binding. This authoritarian leadership style and structure is monarchical, exceedingly unhealthy and contrary to the Gospel teaching of Jesus. It is not fair to the Pope or the people to entrust so much unchecked power to one person. The Spirit after all is given to the whole Church, not just to the Pope, and so the Church's leadership structure ought to reflect this reality.

The fall 2014 synod in Rome received extra news coverage because Pope Francis, in a refreshing change from his predecessors, asked the bishops in attendance to speak openly and candidly even if that meant being in disagreement with the Pope. Several bishops did speak their mind which led to a much more honest and real dialog. But such openness should not be depen-dent on the good will of this or that pope. Honest dialog is a primary means by which the Holy Spirit works in healthy and holy human decision-making.

A key change necessary for structural reform is to require the Pope to be accountable for his use of authority by scaling his authority back from absolute monarch to first among equals in relation to his fellow bishops. Bishops also would become more accountable within their own dioceses. I advocate a decentraliza-tion of church authority from the center in Rome to the local church centered in dioceses. Many more sectors of the Church should be involved in the choosing of popes and bishops and the criteria used in choosing these leaders should be rooted in Gos-pel values. These changes would lessen the possibility of popes and bishops lording it over their people, or getting away with it unchecked when they do.

These changes in the leadership system will guard against the current mentality of popes that leads some of them to hold tight to Church laws and traditions out of respect for past popes instead of out of respect for the people they are called to serve. The disastrous decision of Pope Paul VI in 1968 wherein he held fast to the long held rule against artificial birth control comes to mind as a decision-making process that failed.

Popes of the future should be required to retire at a desig-nated age and also be subject to recall if their job performance is clearly disastrous.

A post structurally reformed Church would be less prone to clericalism, the insidious belief that clergy are holier than lay people. The growing chasm between clergy and laity calls for a declericalized Church leadership. One obvious way to bridge this growing gap would be to allow priests and bishops to marry. A second way would be to allow women to be ordained. These two changes would change the image of the clergy as elite, special, and different from the laity. The only title Jesus definitely used of himself was "son of man" which in his usage means "like a man", i.e., fully human. Priests and bishops are too often perceived as above it all and not subject to the weakness and frailty of the laity.

I can personally attest to the weakness and frailty of priests, starting with myself. I used to think that my struggles to keep my promise of celibacy were atypical. Now I realize that all priests struggle to keep their promise, and many fail because it is not humanly possible or healthy to not love another person emotionally and bodily. There are a rare few who are called to live celibately but they are rare and few indeed. The celibacy system is a tremendous burden to the clergy trying unsuccessfully to live it, and to the people they are called to serve. Clericalism and the mandatory celibacy rule go hand in hand to create an elite caste out of touch with our own humanity and the enfleshed holiness of the laity.

The inclusion of women at all levels of Church leadership would also help to declericalize the priesthood because the other half of the human race would bring completion and balance to the ranks of clergy leaders. The present all-male priesthood creates an unhealthy separation between priests and laity. The addition of women would do wonders for humanizing the priesthood and eliminating its elitist character. But most importantly, the Church desperately needs the talents of women in its leadership ranks. Women deacons, priests and bishops would dramatically improve the quality of leadership in the Catholic Church through gender balance and equality. Male clergy would be more likely to mature psychologically through their experience of working with women as equals.

Another key element in structural reform would be to end the tradition of baptizing infants. The Rite of Christian Initiation of Adults (RCIA) teaches that adult baptism is the norm of Christian initiation; but 99% of Catholics are still baptized as ba-

bies, not adults. De facto, baby baptisms are the norm. The trouble
with this practice is that the RCIA's stress on adult conversion/
transformation is lost in favor of the present system of children
and youth receiving the sacraments of initiation (baptism, eucharist, and confirmation) at prescribed ages. Sacraments are not
rites of magic but celebrations of adult faith. In the Gospels Jesus
calls adults to follow him as disciples, and discipleship requires a
willingness with God's help to enter into a new lifestyle characterized by love, justice and service. Jesus spent his time teaching
adults whereas the Church puts most of its resources into teaching children. Transformation happens primarily by responding to
a call from God to enter into a conscious and chosen relationship
with God through Jesus in the Holy Spirit. This loving relation is
mediated by a community of disciples, by the Word of God, and
by the celebration of the sacraments.

My favorite ministry during my 25 years of active priesthood
was preparing adults for Christian initiation (baptism, confirmation, eucharist/First Communion). It was marvelous to see adults
growing in experiential knowledge of God through faith-sharing,
prayer, and community. Reflection on the stories of Scripture enabled candidates and catechumens to recognize the presence of
God in their own life stories. What often happened though was
that the adults welcomed into the Church at Easter via the sacraments of initiation were not adequately supported by the Church
community because too many of those life-long Catholics were
uneducated in their faith and thus ill- prepared to model discipleship to the newly initiated members of the Church. At the
core of discipleship is not knowing about God but knowing God,
not knowledge about God but experience of God in prayer and
life. At present, the only members of the Church expected to be
disciples of Jesus are the clergy but the clergy face the almost
insuperable obstacles to discipleship of clericalism and celibacy.
Doing away with infant baptism would restore baptism, confir-

mation, and eucharist to their rightful place as signs of adult faith and discipleship.

Jesus did not call children to be his disciples; he called adults. A prerequisite to saying "yes" to Jesus' call to follow him as a disciple was a sense of attraction to Jesus' person and message, and a sense of need for help, for guidance, and inspiration, that is, a need for salvation and redemption, to use traditional religious verbiage. Discipleship in today's world has many negative connotations conjuring up ideas like cults, gurus, and false messiahs. In spite of that, I think it essential to recapture discipleship in the sense it is used in the Gospels so that the baptized identify more with Jesus and the Spirit and less with Church authority and tradition. Imagine thinking of yourself as a disciple of Jesus rather than as a Catholic. At present, there is not even the expectation of discipleship among many Catholics; they equate being Catholic with going to Mass, avoiding sin (mostly sexual sin), and being obedient to the Pope and the bishops. One may be a lifelong Catholic and never know Jesus or the peace he offers freely. Disciples listen to the Word of Jesus and allow it to transform them from within leading them to that peace "which surpasses understanding". A Church engaged in structural reform would place a premium on discipleship and choose leaders who are indeed disciples devoted to Jesus and obedient to his Word.

St. Jerome famously said that "ignorance of Scripture is ignorance of Christ". Another sign of a renewed Church would be adult members whose prayer and faith is strongly rooted in Scripture. Scripture after all is proclaimed by the Church to be the Word of God and so it is the primary means by which one gets to know God. God speaks to us through all of life but in a particularly personal way through Scripture. When a Christian listens to Scripture with faith, the Holy Spirit enables that listening to become a living experience of the presence and voice of God. One of the oldest prayer forms in Christian tradition is "lectio divina" or divine reading. Over time, listening to the Word of God both alone and in community draws the listener into deeper and deeper relation to God and ultimately to contemplation or resting with God in silence. All believers are called by God to contemplation and getting to know Jesus is God's usual way of drawing us into a relationship of trusting love wherein we find the courage to let down our defenses and allow God to change us from within. As things stand now, most Catholics have no expectation of being transformed or illuminated by the Spirit. Too often being Catholic simply means following a set of laws, rules and traditions. What treasures we withhold from believers in Jesus because of ignorance of Scripture. St. Jerome had a point.

The reforms I've enumerated would give the Church a whole new look and feel. Adopting such reforms would require a willingness to let go of the status quo. The greatest obstacle to these changes are clerical and lay leaders who cling tightly to the status quo and refuse to even allow discussion of fundamental changes. They equate current rules and traditions with God's will and lash out at reformers as heretics and dissenters. Reformers are being persecuted left and right for advocating changes. Many reformers have lost their jobs at the hands of bishops and Vatican officials who steadfastly refuse to admit that the current way of doing church is not oriented towards the Kingdom, towards discipleship, towards evangelization, towards critical thinking, or towards a faith that transforms and illumines us into Gospel peace and joy.

Once one sees the vision of what the Church could be, there is no turning back without losing one's way and blocking the Holy Spirit. The Spirit is moving many Catholics to stand up and be counted even if that means being persecuted and marginalized. Jesus' harshest criticism was directed at religious leaders who clung to human traditions over God's priorities of justice, mercy and love. The Catholic Church is becoming a scandal to genuine faith in the world today because of sexual abuse, sexism, authoritarianism and homophobia. The Spirit of the living God will never abandon the Church completely nor allow the status quo to block the flowering of a mature community of disciples immersed in knowledge of God and the fruits of Gospel faith: joy, peace, kindness, love, etc. We need to balance our criticism of the present Church with a vision of what could be if we dare to embark on structural reform.

Chapter Thirty-three

MAINTAINING PERSONAL FAITH
IN A TIME OF DARKNESS

IN EVERY PARISH IN WHICH I SERVED, I came to know people whose faith was intact in spite of crushing losses and hardships. Their intact faith was evident not just from their presence at Mass or involvement in ministry; it was manifest by their gratitude, joy, and love for others. I often marveled at faith that survived such demanding tests.

In particular I remember a woman named Connie who had lost a grown son in a motorcycle accident. When I would chat with her after Mass, I noticed that she had been crying over her tragic loss. But those tearful eyes also exuded a joy and gratitude which moved me deeply. Her faith and love were clearly stronger than death. Connie's ability to persevere in the midst of darkness was an inspiration to me and many others.

I used to marvel at the tested but very much intact faith of many poor immigrants. I was often struck how rapt was the attention of the majority of people at the Spanish Mass in my last parish. Many of these immigrants, who had suffered much to reach the United States and who worked long hours in low paying jobs, exuded a felt need for God in the Scriptures, the sacraments, and in the community of faith. I found it more difficult to take my blessings for granted as I listened to their stories of hardship.

During this time of darkness in the life of the Church, many people seem to have lost their faith while others continue to pray, love and serve, finding their strength and hope in God. The New Testament teaches that faith is a gift from God that cannot be bought, earned or willed. One can lose faith if it is not nurtured but having faith to begin with is a gift.

When I was discerning whether or not to accept a parish assignment after my six month sabbatical in 2004-2005, I found strength and inspiration from individuals and groups who had maintained their dignity and hope under trying circumstances: Nelson Mandela, Aung San Suu Kyi, the Israelites during their seventy year exile, St. Paul, and scores of prophets and saints who continued to praise God in spite of persecution, hardship and want. Although these genuine heroes faced much greater challenges than I, my own challenge felt enormous enough. I felt empowered by others who had followed their consciences and risked exile as a result.

Since I chose exile from priesthood in 2005, my faith has remained intact. Though I nurture my gift of faith with daily prayer, I know that my awareness of God's presence in the people and events of daily life is always a gift. I cannot be too smart for my own good because I am not too smart. I do think a lot about why the Church is in such a crisis these days and I am constantly in search of answers that satisfy my hunger to understand. It's too simple to attribute the Church's problems to the fact that all of us are sinners with an endless capacity for selfishness and myopia. I find more satisfaction from listening to Jesus and watching carefully how he dealt with people especially people who either resisted him and his teaching or were outright hostile to both. His parables alone reveal so much about human frailty, pride and moral blindness. The parable of the Prodigal Son carries an inexhaustible amount of wisdom as it brings to light two human attitudes which vitiate and block faith in the living God: the younger son in the parable sought happiness outside himself in the pleasures and distractions of life; the older son sought happiness through being dutiful, responsible and obedient. Who of us hasn't been there, done that. The temptation of the older son may be more difficult to overcome because he equated faith with keeping the commandments and obeying the rules. It is such an easy trap for anyone drawn to religion to think that God's love and approval can be earned.

In my experience, faith that lasts is built on an experience of God's overwhelming love, mercy and compassion. In other words, faith endures when a believer understands experientially the New Testament's claim that what is most important is not that we love God but that God loves us, and that all our efforts to love and please God are a response to God having first loved us, continuing to love us now, and promising to love us forever unto eternal life.

To open ourselves to God's loving presence is difficult in any time or place but particularly challenging in our noisy, distracted and materialistic era. A great rediscovery in the late 20th century is the mystical tradition of the Catholic faith. Writers and teachers such as Thomas Merton, Thomas Keating, and Anthony de Mello remind us that we are all called to become contemplatives; that there is no substitute for experience of God in love. In the end, only God's loving presence can keep us sane and hopeful through the trials and tribulations of life. The Holy Spirit seeks to lead us step by step into daily contemplation wherein we seek the face of God in silence, trust and humility. The courage and patience to embark on the contemplative journey is communicated through the friendship of Jesus who takes us where we are and as we are, with all our weaknesses and limitations. When we grow discouraged and depleted, Jesus encourages us with the reminder that it is he who chose us, not we who chose him. Direct experience of God is the one sure foundation for maintaining faith in times of darkness.

Sex abuse survivors frequently lose their capacity for faith altogether because at the time they were sexually assaulted by a priest or religious brother or sister, their faith was not sufficiently developed to withstand the trauma they experienced. Learning to trust anyone, much less God, is one of the great challenges for abuse survivors. My own experience of Catholic leaders, as described throughout this book, leads me to share the conviction of most abuse survivors that these leaders are not worthy of trust because so many continue to lie, scapegoat, and minimize the horrendous crimes perpetrated against children and youth in Catholic parishes and schools throughout the world. Abuse survivors need to see the institutional Church embark on structural reform which results in transparency and accountability at all levels of decision making and Church life. Then, maybe abuse survivors can begin to trust in the Word of God proclaimed by the Church through its bishops, priests, deacons, and lay leaders. That goal is my heart's desire and my urgent prayer.

Chapter Thirty-four

"MAKE COMMON CAUSE
WITH THE LOSERS"

IN THE 2009 BOOK "Mountains Beyond Mountains, One Doctor's Quest to Heal the World", by Tracy Kidder, Dr. Paul Farmer is quoted: "I have fought for my whole life a long defeat. . .what we're really trying to do . . .is make common cause with the losers". (p. 288). The "losers" to whom Dr. Farmer alludes are the poor of Haiti. That same sentiment could apply to the life and work of Jesus who lived in solidarity with the "losers" of his day and suffered defeat by crucifixion for his efforts.

The priesthood into which I was ordained in 1979 and from which I exiled myself in 2005 made it very difficult to "make common cause with the losers". Priests are winners by the clerical culture into which they are ordained. Priests, until recently, garnered instant respect from people inside and outside the Church. Addressed as "father" by all and set apart by distinctive dress and a secure living, priests find it very difficult to make common cause with the losers of this world. Priests become accustomed to being the center of attention and of garnering automatic respect and deference. The mystique of professed celibacy adds to a priest's star power. Some priests know that abuse survivors, women and gay people are treated shamefully by the Church hierarchy but the majority of priests do not dare risk their status and livelihood to make common cause with those who suffer so unjustly. From my observation, most priests do not self identify as followers/ disciples of Jesus, so Jesus' call to discipleship is not the standard by which they understand their calling.

Following Jesus as his disciple is a call to downward mobility whereas becoming a priest is a path to upward mobility. The priest is freed from the challenge of making a living, the challenge of rearing a family, and the challenge to grow up emotionally through the intimacy of marriage. There are mature priests but studies and the experience of many lay people indicate they are the exception, not the norm.

In 2012, only one man was to be ordained priest for the Archdiocese of New York. I read a story about him in the New York Times in which he spoke of how humbled he is to joining such a holy profession. I felt enormous pity for him because he has been set up for failure, frustration and loneliness by an institution in total denial about the failed state of its leadership structure. The stories I have told in this book reveal an institution in decline led by men who are incapable of reforming the crumbling structure that is the institutional Catholic Church. That incapacity was captured in the words of Bishop Allen Vigneron to me in 2005 to the effect that he did not see any need for structural reform in the Catholic Church.

In early 2013, a new Pope was chosen to lead the universal Church. In May 2013, a new priest named Father Michael Barber was named by the Pope to be the next Bishop of Oakland. These changes give many people hope that maybe this time, things will be different. On Sunday, May 5th, 2013, while I was standing outside the Oakland Cathedral with sign in hand, a Spanish speaking man from my last parish assignment in Fremont, Corpus Christi, stopped by to say hello. He asked me what I thought of the new Pope. I told him I was happy a Latino had been chosen. He replied that the Pope's ethnicity was secondary to him. I said I was encouraged by the apparent simple lifestyle of Pope Francis and of his commitment to the poor. At hearing this, the man's face lit up and he expressed his joy at the prospect of a servant leader as opposed to so many who expect to be treated as royalty. I marveled at the simple wisdom of this Mexican immigrant who understands and believes in Jesus' first requirement of Church leaders: that they be committed to serve, not to being served.

The Catholic Church's leadership has lost its way and its credibility in the world due to its clericalism, its refusal to treat women as equals, and its ongoing insistence on mandatory celibacy for priests, and most egregiously, its failure to put the protection of children ahead of protecting the image and money of the Church. The Spirit which Jesus promised his disciples before disappearing from their sight is working inside and outside the Church to bring about fundamental changes. The status quo is crumbling at the edges as more and more believers and non-believers cry out, ENOUGH IS ENOUGH.

Jesus doesn't ask us to be winners but he does call us to be faithful because God is worthy of our trust and the Kingdom of God will one day triumph over all its counterfeits. In the meantime, I plan to strive every day to stay in solidarity with those who suffer exclusion on the margins of the Church and to stay in touch day by day with Spirit of the living God. I hope you will join me in "making common cause with the losers." The "losers" of every time and place are the poor and those who are not getting a fair shake. In today's Church, the losers are sexual abuse survivors, women, and gay and lesbian people. They need and deserve our friendship and support so they may take their rightful place in the Eucharistic assembly each Sunday. May we all stand in solidarity with them until that blessed day happens.

CPSIA information can be obtained
at www.ICGtesting.com
Printed in the USA
FSOW01n1805050315
5507FS